FROM THE PIT TO THE PRISON TO THE PALACE

"Unto thee will I cry, O LORD my rock; be not silent to me: lest, if thou be silent to me, I become like them that go down into the pit."
—Psalm 28:1

FIDEL M. DONALDSON

From the Pit to the Prison to the Palace
By Fidel M. Donaldson
Copyright © 2010 Appeal Ministries

Unless otherwise stated, quotations from the Bible are from the King James Version.

ISBN: 978-0-9827710-0-6

LCCN: 2010907252

Printed in the United States of America

ACKNOWLEDGEMENTS

This book is dedicated to King Jesus: The Author and Finisher of my faith. He brought me out of a horrible pit, out of the miry clay, and set my feet upon a rock.

Much Love To: My mom and Dad for never giving up on me; my precious wife for life, Paulette, and all our children; my sister Janet, who prays for me and supports the ministry.

I thank the Lord Jesus for the Intercessors who have prayed for me over the years, for the men and women who have mentored me: Bishop James Ferguson and Dr. Lillian Ferguson. Reverend Andre Cook. Special thanks to my spiritual parents: Pastor Samuel and Pastor Katie Greene. My Church family: Narrow Way Ministries. The members of Appeal Ministries and The SWAT Team (Soldiers Watching And Travailing).

A special thanks to Dr. Tassel Daley for editing the manuscript. Mr. Chad Schapiro for encouraging and motivating me.

TABLE OF CONTENTS

PREFACE

Hindsight allows us to look back over our lives to see the decisions we made and to understand the repercussions of those decisions. Once we gain an understanding, we can use the wisdom to make better decisions. As I look back over my life, I can readily see that I was in the pit of sin and despair because I was in rebellion against God. The lifestyle I lived was all about pleasing the flesh. I was powerless to change that lifestyle because I was under the control of my carnal nature. Once Jesus opened my eyes, I was able to see the devastation sin had caused, the prison sentence I had to serve, and the pit of despair into which sin had plunged me.

When Jesus rescued me, I made a vow to surrender my life to Him so He could use me as an instrument of deliverance for others. God is merciful and full of grace. He has provided a way out of the pit, and that way is through His Son Jesus Christ. God has given me the grace to chronicle my deliverance in several books. My desire is that this book will be a source of hope and inspiration to others who have fallen into a pit because of sinful actions. I pray that it will inspire and encourage people to reach out and help someone else out of their pit, their prison, and out of any other place of bondage.

This book contains my testimony of deliverance from a lifestyle of drug dealing, drunkenness, and fornication. It chronicles a lifestyle that led me to an eight year prison sentence in an English prison. It was a prison located next to a pig farm. It chronicles a lifestyle that brought pain to my wife and children when they had to struggle to survive while I was running the streets—neglecting my responsibilities as husband and father. It chronicles how my life was changed when Jesus revealed Himself to me and washed me in His blood.

Revelation 12:11 declares, *"And they overcame him by the blood of the Lamb, and by the word of their testimony; and they loved not their lives unto the death."* I have a testimony because Jesus spared my life, and this book contains that testimony. If this book reaches the hands of one person on drugs, one person in prison, one person trapped in the pit and the bondage of sin, it will have accomplished its purpose. Through this book, I want the reader to know there is no pit that is so deep, no place that is so dark, no prison that is so fortified that the Lord Jesus cannot pull them out, shine His light, and set them free.

FOREWORD

He lifted me out of the mire clay. He planted my feet on a Rock to stay. He placed a song in my heart to sing. A song of praise, Hallelujah!

"God is in the lifting up business." It does not matter what situation you are in. It does not matter how you got in the situation. God has provided a way of escape.

Joseph was placed in a pit because of his jealous brothers. Job was in distress because he was an upright man, and the devil wanted him to curse God. The author of this book was placed in prison because of wrong doings. In all three cases, God lifted them out of their pit.

From the Pit to the Prison to the Palace is a book of hope. It describes the benefits of prayer, praise, and thanksgiving. When the author's wife told him that one day he would be preaching the gospel, he laughed. Today, not only is he preaching the gospel but he is also the author of several life changing books.

There is hope for the hopeless. The Gideon Bible Society is famous for leaving Bibles in hotels, prisons, and other places. These Bibles have literally changed the lives of many, including the author of this book. By placing copies of this book in prisons, hospitals, and other places, the lives of many will also be changed. Whom the Lord loveth, He chasteneth. Read the life story of Fidel Donaldson as related in this book. The Lord is no respecter of persons. *From the Pit to the Prison to the Palace* will keep your eyes riveted to its pages until you read the last line. You will never be the same after reading this book.

Remember, what the devil meant for evil, God will work for Good. Read this book!

Dr. Tassel Daley

CHAPTER 1

The Pit

"And they took him, and cast him into a pit: and the pit was empty, there was no water in it" (Genesis 37:24).

Life is full of pits and pitfalls. Someone once said, "If life is a bowl of cherries then why do I feel like the pits?" I believe most of the pits and the pitfalls into which people fall are due to bad decisions, betrayal by others, or as my Pastor Dr. Samuel Greene stated, "The dealings of God." Whatever the reason for your present pit, you can take solace in the fact that the Lord will pull you out if you allow him to. When the Lord pulls you out you will be in a better state than when you went in. I was commenting to a friend the other day on how we have to face one obstacle after another. As soon as one is overcome, here comes another. Sometimes, a new obstacle arrives while we are dealing with the current one. It is akin to a long distance race with many hurdles. As soon as the athlete gets over one hurdle, he has a short respite before he has to prepare to get over the next. We have to be patient and wait on the Lord for deliverance.

David said, *"I waited on the LORD; and he inclined unto me, and heard my cry. He brought me up also out of a horrible pit, out of the mire clay, and set my feet upon a rock, and established my goings. And he hath put a new song in my mouth, even praise unto our God: Many shall see it, and fear, and shall trust in the LORD" (Psalms 40: 1-3).* It is bad enough to be in a pit, but when it is a horrible pit, it is worse. David did not take matters into his own hands but instead he trusted in the LORD and cried unto HIM. If you learn to praise Jesus in the pit, He will give you a new song. God set his feet upon a rock, and He will do the same for you. Jesus is the solid rock upon which we must stand. Once we are standing on the solid rock, He will establish and direct our path. When the LORD brings you out of the pit, when He helps you to overcome the obstacle or the hurdle, it will be evident to all—even to those who wished for your demise. Many will trust in the LORD because your deliverance will be tangible evidence to them that God is real and He is on your side.

I've been in some pits throughout the course of my life, and I fell into a horrible one in the month of November in the year 1990. I was in a house with a lot of cocaine, and the police were pounding down the door. That pit was used by the Lord Jesus to bring me into a covenant relationship with Him. I will give more details on my personal pit experience in prison later.

God's desire for every human being is for them to receive salvation by grace through faith. This is made possible by the finished work of Jesus Christ on the cross of Calvary and His resurrection from the grave. Salvation is not an end in itself but a means to an end. The end is God bringing those that He has saved to a place of perfection in Him. The purpose of this perfection is to have a people who can carry His Glory. Attaining perfection through Christ should be the goal of every born again believer. Perfection can and will be achieved when we have been completely delivered from our sin nature. I believe many people are intimidated when they hear the word perfection because they feel it is impossible to reach such a lofty goal, but God would not tell us to be perfect as He is perfect if perfection were not attainable. Please remember that with God, all things are possible, and it is important to understand the Biblical definition of the word perfect. *"And when Abram was ninety years old and nine, the LORD appeared to Abram, and said unto him, I am the Almighty God; walk before me, and be thou perfect" (Genesis 17:1).*

The Hebrew word for perfect, as it is used here, is tamiym (pronounced taw-meem), and it means *integrity, truth,* and *wholeness.* It is indicative of the person who has come to a place of maturity in Jesus Christ. We should be encouraged by the fact that Abram was ninety-nine when he received the word on perfection from the Lord. Our encouragement should come from the fact that it is a lifelong process, and God will finish the work He has begun in us. He is called the father of the faithful, but he hit some bumps along the road in his pursuit of perfection. Concerning Noah, the Bible says, *"Noah was a just man and perfect in his generations, and Noah walked with God" (Genesis 6:9b).* Do not become discouraged and quit if you mess up. Repent when you fall. Get up and get back on the narrow road. Do not take a step back when you experience setback because God is working on your comeback. He turns stumbling blocks into stepping stones. He makes your latter days greater and more productive than your former. As we yield to the Holy Ghost, He shows us the things in our lives that are hindering our walk with God. With the Holy Ghost on the inside of us, and the constant washing of the word, we will reach that place of maturity in Him.

Before we can reach the place of Divine perfection, we must be brought out of the pit of sin into which Adam's rebellion caused us to fall. The life of Joseph gives us a snapshot of how God will take us from the pit to the prison to the palace. The palace is synonymous with the Kingdom of God.

When you study the life of Joseph, you see an individual who never murmured or complained throughout his pit, his betrayal in Potiphar's house, or his prison experience. His life is a great example of how we should trust God no matter how difficult the pit may be. Joseph did not wind up in the pit because of any outward sin that he committed. He was the victim of brothers who were envious of his relationship with his father. For Joseph, the pit experience was used by God to process him for promotion and to prepare him to preserve posterity for His people. If we allow Him to, God will use our pit experiences to help others who have fallen into a pit of their own, but we must allow Him to take us out. Don't beat upon yourself if you have fallen into a pit. Sometimes God will allow us to be there to prepare us for something great.

At seventeen years of age, Joseph already had a revelation that he would be used by God. Like most seventeen-year-olds, he was a bit cocky and brash. He was the favorite son and was given a coat of many colors by his father. The obvious favoritism did not sit well with his brothers. His relationship with his brothers was worsened by the fact that he brought his father news of their evil deeds. *"And when his brethren saw that his father loved him more than all his brethren, they hated him, and could not speak peaceably unto him" (Genesis 37:4).*

Have you ever lived in a home where one of your siblings was the favorite and could do no wrong in the eyes of your parents? To make matters worse, your sibling was a tattletale who told your parents everything that you did. The tension between Joseph and his brothers was exacerbated by his revelation to them of a dream that he had. When God reveals things to us in dreams and visions, we must be careful with whom we share them because there are dream and vision killers out there who do not want to see our dreams manifest. They would like nothing more than to see the dream become a nightmare. I know we like to share what the Lord is doing in our lives with others, but before the Lord brings the dream or vision to pass in our lives, it is better to keep a tight lip. God has a plan for your life, and the devil will stop at nothing to see that plan aborted. He will use anything and anyone to stop that plan from being birthed. In many instances, we are our worst enemies because of our inability to keep our mouths shut. The devil cannot read our minds, so he waits for us to give him the ammunition he needs. He is the prince of the power of the air, and he and his minions are seeking opportunities to use our words and our actions against us.

Joseph would find out what was in the heart of his brothers once he revealed the dream to them. It was bad enough his brothers hated him, but because of the dream the Bible says, *"They hated him yet the more."* There are people who are not going to like you just because of the favor of the Father on your life. They will dislike you even more when that favor begins to manifest, but don't be angry with them. There is a spirit that is using them to fight against you.

When God gives us a revelation of a work He will do in our lives, we have to wait on His timing because He has to take us to a place of preparation to facilitate the fulfillment of that revelation. Most people can attest to the fact that the place of preparation will not be a bed of roses. When you search the scriptures and study the lives of the individuals whom God used to do a great work in their generation, you will notice one common denominator. The common denominator is the fact that they were all tested and tried. Abraham was a stranger in the land of promise and had to dwell in tabernacles with his son Isaac and his grandson Jacob. Moses was raised up in the lap of luxury in Egypt, but he was tending sheep in a desert when the Lord called him. The Bible says, *"Choosing rather to suffer affliction with the people of God, than to enjoy the pleasures of sin for a season; Esteeming the reproach of Christ greater riches than the treasures in Egypt for he had respect unto the recompence of the reward" (Hebrews 11:25-26).* Our suffering in this life is not in vain, for if we suffer with Him, we will reign with Him. The pleasures of sin are only for a season, but the blessings we will receive when we pick up our cross and follow Jesus will be for eternity.

David was anointed to be king, but he had to run for his life because King Saul wanted to kill him. He went through various pit experiences before he was able to be seated on the throne. He wound up depressed, dwelling in caves and in the land of the Philistines. If someone expects to be used by God, they have to be willing to endure testing and trials.

God had a plan to do great things in the life of Joseph. The plan included the pit, the prison, and Potiphar's house. Many people desire to get to the palace, but the process of preparation cannot be circumvented. If you want to have a mediocre life in Christ, then you can sit on the fence of indecision; but if you are willing to be processed for promotion, then surrender to the Lord and allow His will to be done in your life. Jesus has to be the captain of your ship if you want Him to take you to the destination He has charted for your life. God charted a destination for young Joseph, and his journey started when he dreamed.

With youthful exuberance, Joseph let the proverbial cat out of the bag by telling his brothers that in his dream, they would do obeisance before him; that revelation did not sit well with them at all. Joseph's next dream brought a rebuke from his father because in that dream it was not only his brothers that were doing obeisance before him but also his parents. The word obeisance in Hebrew is *shachah.* The word *shachah* means *to prostrate in homage to royalty or God, to crouch, to fall down flat, to reverence.* With that definition, you can see why Joseph's brothers were not enamored with his dreams and desired to rid him from their lives.

5

God had a plan for Joseph's life, but at seventeen, he could not fully comprehend that plan or how God would fulfill it. I believe if God had allowed him to see the process he would go through, he probably would have kept his mouth shut and asked for the cup of bitterness to pass. It appears that God does not reveal His total plan to us at once because we would not be able to handle it. The prophet Jeremiah was told by God, *"Before I formed thee in the belly I knew thee; and before thou camest forth out of the womb I sanctified thee, and I ordained thee a prophet unto the nations" (Jeremiah 1:5).* Joseph was given a dream at seventeen, but Jeremiah was called from the womb. Can you imagine being sanctified or set apart and ordained as a prophet to the nations before you come out of the womb? Jeremiah was probably overjoyed with such a glowing prophecy, but after a while, he realized that the people to whom he had to prophesy were not too happy with him or the words that he prophesied. Once he started to deliver the prophetic word to the people concerning the Babylonian captivity, he came under attack and derision. He was smacked in the face by Pashur and put in stocks near the house of the Lord. What irony—the prophet to the nations was getting slapped around and thrown in jail, and to add insult to injury, the jail was next to the House of the Lord.

The title prophet is thrown around frivolously today because most people get glowing prophecies on how many blessings they will receive. Before Jeremiah could give a prophecy on restoration, he first had to tell the people of their captivity. The people were in no mood to hear about captivity, and Jeremiah felt the brunt of disgust at his prophetic utterances. Jeremiah spoke to the LORD and said, *"O Lord, thou hast deceived me, and I was deceived: thou art stronger than I, and hast prevailed: I am in derision daily, every one mocketh me. For since I spake, I cried out, I cried violence and spoil; because the word of the LORD was made a reproach unto me, and a derision, daily"* (Jeremiah 20: 7-8).

God has a plan for your life, just like He had a plan for Joseph's life, and just like He had a plan for Jeremiah's life. The truth is not an easy pill to swallow, and you will be attacked for speaking it, but you must stand on the Word of God when you are mocked and criticized for speaking the word of the Lord. If you are in the pit right now, you must continue to trust the sovereignty of God because He knows exactly where you are and how long you will be there. You may be in a pit of despair because of the betrayal of a husband, a wife, or even someone in the church, but I encourage you to hold on because many of God's great leaders had to be delivered from the pit of despair.

Remember, King David was in such despair over Saul's jealous attempts on his life that he decided to leave his people and dwell in the land of the Philistines. You know you are in a serious pit when the world looks more attractive to you than the people of God. David was able to survive because he found a way to encourage himself in the Lord his God. Some of the greatest attacks we have to face will come from people who are close to us. David said, *"Yea, mine own familiar friend, in whom I trusted, which did eat of my bread, hath lifted up his heel against me" (Psalm 41: 9).* He went on to say, *"But thou O LORD, be merciful unto me, and raise me up, that I may requite them. By this I know that thou favourest me, because mine enemy doth not triumph over me" (Psalm 49: 10-11).* Many believers pray for the favor of God but must realize there are times when His favor brings trials. It is like praying for patience. When we pray for patience, God will allow things to happen that will both test and teach us patience. *"My brethren, count it all joy when ye fall into divers temptations; Knowing this, that the trying of your faith worketh patience. But let patience have her perfect work, that ye may be perfect and entire, wanting nothing" (James 1:2-4).* David asked the LORD to raise him up because he knew God's favor was on his life, and with that favour he would always triumph over his enemies. Stand strong because the favour of God on your life will cause you to rise from the pit of despair, and cause you to triumph over your enemies.

Joseph's brothers hated him so much that they conspired to kill him. It's really the dream they were trying to kill. It's not really you the enemy wants to kill. He is after God's dream, His vision for your life. The enemy wants to destroy the plan of God for your life, and he will use anybody to do it—even people in your own family. The devil is so crafty he will even use us against ourselves. He loves to make us believe God has forgotten us in our trials, or God is keeping something good from us. That is the tactic he used on Eve in the great deception. He convinced her that God did not want her to eat of the fruit of the tree because if she did, her eyes would be opened and she would be like God. He did not tell her the consequences of disobeying the Word of God. In Joseph's case it was his brothers the enemy would use to try to destroy him, but God would use their plan for his good.

Joseph was sent by his father to check on his brothers, and when they saw him from afar they said, *"Behold, this dreamer cometh" (Genesis 37:19).* They identified him as a dreamer because they knew that he knew there was more to his future than tending to the flocks in the field. Beloved, never lose sight of your dream no matter how reviled or criticized you are for it. People might hate you because God has shown you what He is going to do in your life, but do not allow the haters to hinder you. Believe me when I tell you that people can see your potential in God. You might only be able to see your shortcomings and the things you lack, but others can see beyond the surface and know that God is going to do some special things with your life.

There is a story recorded in 1 Samuel 18 about David upon his return from the slaughter of the Philistines. On David's return, the women came out of all cities of Israel singing and dancing. They came out to meet King Saul but were singing and dancing about David's military prowess. *"And the women answered one another as they played, and said, Saul hath slain his thousands, and David his ten thousands" (1 Samuel 18:7).* Saul was very wroth about the accolades David received from the women and recognized that David was next in line to be King. Verse 9 of 1 Samuel 18 says, *"And Saul eyed David from that day and forward."* It is ironic that many years later, Saul's daughter Michal would do the very same thing. *"And as the ark of the LORD came into the city of Daivd, Michal Saul's daughter looked through a window, and saw king David leaping and dancing before the LORD; and she despised him in her heart" (2 Samuel 6:16).* Why would anyone despise someone else for leaping and dancing before the LORD? They do it because there is a seed of jealousy in their heart. She should have joined her husband in the celebration, but instead she is peeping through a window with a heart that is riddled with jealousy. Because of the condition of her heart, she was barren and could not reproduce.

We have a difficult time comprehending God's plan for our lives because the plan usually involves testing and trials, which God uses to strengthen our faith and mature us. The tests and the trials are more difficult when the people who come against us are those whom we expect to have our best interest at heart. Remember that it was the disciple who carried the money bag who betrayed Jesus with a kiss. In the midst of the betrayal of a close associate, try to remember that God will work it into His plan for your life. God told Jeremiah, *"For I know the thoughts that I think toward you, saith the LORD, thoughts of peace, and not of evil, to give you an expected end. Then shall you call upon me, and you shall go and pray unto me, and I will hearken unto you. And you shall seek me, and find me, when you shall search for me with all your heart"* (Jeremiah 29: 11-13).

God has a good plan for us, a plan of peace and not of evil, a plan to prosper us. He wants us to call upon him through prayer. The trials that He allows to come into our lives are for the purpose of teaching us to focus on Him. Don't be discouraged by the trials you are facing at the moment. You might not be able to see your way out at the present time, but the people around you can see the fact that despite all your failures, God has a plan to prosper you. You can look beyond your current circumstances and know for a surety that your expected end in God is great. Do not allow your troubles to cause you to turn away from Him. Call upon God and seek Him while He may be found. He wants you to search for Him with your whole heart. Just like Joseph, God's favor is upon you, but there is a process you must endure to walk in that favor. Joseph's brothers could recognize him from afar because they could see the coat of many colors from a distance. The coat was a continual reminder to them of the father's favor on his life. Your praise is your coat of many colors, and when your brothers in Christ Jesus see you praising God in the furnace of your affliction, they will see that He has given you the garment of praise for the spirit of heaviness. The devil can see your coat of praise, and he knows your position in God. That is why he wants to strip you of that coat and put you in a coat of heaviness.

Do not be deterred by the fact that the enemy will use people close to you to derail your destiny and plunge you into a pit of despair. When someone close to us betrays us, that betrayal is especially difficult to deal with. David said, *"For it was not an enemy that reproached me; then I could have borne it: neither was it he that hated me that did magnify himself against me; then I would have hid myself from him: But it was thou, a man mine equal, my guide, and mine acquaintance. We took sweet counsel together, and walked unto the house of God in company" (Psalms 55: 12-14).* I heard someone say, "You have not experienced hurt until you have experienced church hurt." I learned that first hand when I saw the pain my wife suffered when I ran the streets and neglected her. There are many individuals that are carrying scars from the past betrayal of a wife, husband, a brother or sister in Christ, or someone they trusted. Remember, man's feet are made of clay, so put your trust in God and not man. People will fail us, but Jesus never fails.

Joseph's brothers said, *"Come now therefore, and let us slay him, and cast him into some pit, and we will say, some evil beast hath devoured him: and we shall see what will become of his dreams" (Genesis 37: 20).* Notice their devious plan is birthed out of their desire to kill the dream. Stopping the dream from coming to fruition was the focal point of their plan. The devil and his demons send major attacks against the carriers of the plan of God. The devil will attempt to use the pit as a place to destroy the dream, but God will use the pit as a processing hub to position you for your promotion. Joseph's brothers were convinced that the pit would be the perfect place to kill the dream, but there is no pit or place that is so deep that God can't reach down and pull you out. The same pit the enemy has dug for you, God will use to perfect praise in you, to mature you, to push you to a place where you can fulfill His plan for your life.

"And it came to pass when Joseph was come unto his brethren, that they stripped Joseph out of his coat, his coat of many colors that was on him; and they took him, and cast him into a pit: and the pit was empty, there was no water in it" (Genesis 37:23).

Notice the first thing they did was they stripped him of his coat. This meant he had no covering and no outward evidence of favor with his earthly father. No water in the pit meant he was in a dry place. While Joseph was in the pit, Judah spoke to his brothers and convinced them not to kill him but to sell him. He was sold to some Ishmeelites traders for twenty pieces of silver, and they took him to Egypt. His journey to Egypt meant he had to travel thirty days through the desert. Thirty is the number of consecration and maturity or preparation for ministry. The desert is a symbol of desolation, temptation, and solitude. In order to consecrate us, to mature us, and to prepare us for our ministry, God will allow us to go through some dry and desolate places, but we must trust Him to bring us out. Remember, it was the Spirit who led or drove Jesus into the wilderness or desert to be tempted by the devil. It was God who pointed out Job to Satan and asked him, *"Have you considered my servant Job?"* Take courage in the fact that if God points you out, or leads you to a solitary place to be tested, it is because He knows you can handle the furnace.

God was transforming Joseph from a brash, bragging seventeen-year-old to a mature leader who could carry the Glory and help nations. Joseph was sold into slavery in Egypt and had to go through a desert or wilderness to get there, and the nation of Israel would be slaves in Egypt and would have to travel through a desert or wilderness after leaving Egypt. Believers were brought out of Egypt and had to go through a wilderness to be processed for their ultimate promotion to perfection. No believer is exempt from the wilderness or desert experience; we are either coming out or going in. The Apostle Paul wrote two thirds of the New Testament, but when he was called by Jesus, he went in the desert of Arabia for a season to be with the LORD.

The purpose of the wilderness is found in *Deuteronomy 8:2*. In speaking to the nation of Israel, Moses said, *"And thou shalt remember all the way which the LORD thy God led thee these forty years in the wilderness, to humble thee, and to prove thee, to know what was in thine heart whether thou wouldest keep his commandments, or no."* The Hebrew word for prove is *nacah* (pronounced *naw-saw*), and it means *to test, to try, or to tempt.* The wilderness will expose the things in our heart so God can deal with those things. We all have things in our hearts that need to be cut away. That is the reason why our hearts have to be circumcised. There are people who are not guilty of what I call major sins—such as murder, rape, or assault—but those people might have issues in their hearts, such as lust, unforgiveness, self-righteousness, or even covetousness. These things have to be dealt with. I love when I hear people say, *"The Lord knows my heart."* I respond by saying, *"The heart is deceitful above all things, and is desperately wicked: who can know it?" (Jeremiah 17:9).* I will tell you who can know the deceitful, desperate, wicked heart of a man: God knows it.

To the Hebrew, the heart is the center of the man, so the Bible is saying that man at his center, at the very core of his being, is deceitful above all things and desperately wicked. God will use the desert or the wilderness to purge and to prune us of our wicked hearts. Jesus was without sin and had a heart that was completely given over to His Father, but as a man, He did not exempt Himself from the wilderness experience, so why do we think we should get an exemption? On our journey of faith, we will spend time in various wildernesses or deserts; it is a matter of when, not if. Before God promotes us, we will have to spend the allotted time. The length of our time spent in the wilderness will be determined by how we conduct ourselves. The more we murmur and complain, the longer we stay.

The Israelites wandering in the wilderness and how they conducted themselves should be a lesson to all of us. God does not inhabit the murmuring of His people; He inhabits their praises. You'd better praise Him in the wilderness because your praise is your ticket out.

Jesus was thirty years old when He came to the Jordan to be baptized by John, and He was led into a desert or wilderness to be tempted by the devil. Ezekiel was a captive in Babylon, and in the thirtieth year of his life, he was prepared for his ministry with a series of apocalyptic visions of God. Like Jesus, like Joseph, and like Ezekiel, you and I will have to go through a process of preparation for the ministry God has for us; the greater the ministry, the greater the process. Do not envy anyone with a large, prosperous ministry because you do not know what they had to endure to get to that place. God does not give happy meal trials for steak and lobster blessings. The test is always commensurate with the level of promotion. If you desire the promotion, then you must be willing to withstand the test. Where do you think testimonies come from? They come from the tests you and I pass. Stand firm because you will pass the current test with flying colors.

The selling of Joseph into slavery was meant for evil by his brothers, but God would use Egypt as the place where Joseph's dreams would manifest. Please remember that Joseph had to go through the desert—the dry, solitary place—to get to Egypt, the place of further testing and manifestation. In Egypt, he would have to endure more hardships, such as the false accusations of sexual assault by Potiphar's wife and the subsequent prison sentence that followed. Joseph is our example of how God will be with us even in the most difficult places. Joseph was tested and tried, but he never complained. He waited on the manifestation of the Word of God in his life. Concerning Joseph, the Bible says, *"Until the time that his word came: the word of the LORD tried him" (Psalm 105:19).* Until the manifestation of a specific word in his life, Joseph was tried by the word of the LORD.

God has a proceeding word for each of us, but until it comes, the Word of God will try us in order to get us ready to walk in the proceeding Word. The Hebrew word for tried is *tsaraph* (pronounced *tsaw-raf*), and it means *to refine, to melt, to purge away.* It has the connotation of a gold or silversmith working with the gold and the silver until they are purified. Our perfection as believers will come through the purifying fire of God. The majority of the time that I hear scriptures read from the book of Malachi, it is always the portion on robbing God in tithes and offerings, but there is much more to this book. It is about God purifying the priesthood. *"And he shall sit as refiner and purifier of silver: and he shall purify the sons of Levi, and purge them as gold and silver, that they may offer unto the LORD an offering in righteousness. Then shall the offering of Judah and Jerusalem be pleasant unto the LORD, as in the days of old, and as in the former years" (Malachi 3:3-4).*

A friend sent me a story called *The Silversmith. "There was a group of women in a Bible study on the book of Malachi. As they were studying Chapter three, they came across verse three which says, 'He will sit as a refiner and purifier of silver.' This verse puzzled the women and they wondered what this statement meant about the character and nature of God. One of the women offered to find out about the process of refining silver to report to the group at their next Bible study session.*

"That week this woman called up a silversmith and made an appointment to watch him at work. She didn't mention anything

about the reason for her interest in silver beyond her curiosity about the process of refining silver. As she watched the silver smith, he held a piece of silver over the fire and let it heat up. He explained that in refining silver, one needed to hold the silver in the middle of the fire where the flames were hottest so as to burn away all the impurities.

"The woman thought about God holding us in such a hot spot then she thought again about the verse that says, 'He sits as a refiner and purifier of silver.' She asked the silversmith if it was true that he had to sit there in front of the fire the whole time the silver was being refined. The man answered that yes, he not only had to sit there holding the silver, but he had to keep his eyes on the silver the entire time it was in the fire. For, if the silver was left even a moment too long in the flames, it would be destroyed. The woman was silent for a moment. Then she asked the silversmith, 'How do you know when the silver is fully refined?' He smiled at her and answered, 'Oh, that's the easy part, when I see my image reflected in it.' The story went on to say, 'If today you are feeling the heat of the fire, remember that God has His eyes on you and will keep His hand on you and watch over you until He sees His image in you.'" His eyes are on the sparrow, and I know He watches me. Hallelujah!!!

God's place of preparation for the manifestation of the dreams He has given us is not a comfortable place. It is a place of trials, a place of stretching, and a place where we have to take our eyes off our surroundings and look to Him. In order to get us to the place of purpose, God will use whatever means He deems necessary. Sometimes, He will allow our sins to take us to a place where we have no choice but to cry out to Him. For me, that place was a prison cell; for others, it may have been from drug rehab or even from a divorce that stemmed from adultery or emotional or physical abuse. Whatever or wherever the pit is, know that God is trying to get your attention.

Joseph's dreams were the catalyst that propelled him to his place of purpose, destiny, and divine assignment. It does not appear that we learn our greatest lessons when things are going well; on the contrary, it appears that it is out of adversity that we learn and grow. Muscles are not built when we are relaxing on the couch watching a good movie; muscles are built through resistance and repetition. Faith is like a muscle in that the more we exercise it, the stronger it becomes. If you have been thrown in a pit by someone close to you or by some self-inflicted wound, do not allow despair to drive you deeper. The number one rule of holes is, when you are in one, stop digging.

CHAPTER 2

The Pruning Process

When my wife and I moved into our home, we inherited seven citrus trees, which included four orange trees, one lemon tree, one grapefruit tree, and a tangerine tree. I have always loved fruits because as a child, growing up in Jamaica, there were many tropical fruits. When I moved to New York City, there was a pear tree on the lot next to our house, but it could not be compared to the delicious fruits upon which I feasted as a child growing up in Jamaica.

I was excited about having so many citrus trees on our property, and we eagerly looked forward to the time when the fruits would ripen and the juices could be extracted. I did not realize that at a certain time of the year, the trees needed to be pruned so the next season's crop would be more bountiful. A family member came by and informed me of the pruning process. I remember watching as he pruned one of the tress; he cut it so far back I thought he was going to cut it down. He alleviated my fears by letting me know that the process was beneficial for the tree.

In order for the trees to be more productive, they had to be pruned. I must admit that eating the fruits was much more enjoyable than the labor that went into the pruning. Pruning seven trees is very labor intensive, but the prospect of getting more delicious fruits gave me the energy to press on. I learned a painful lesson from the lemon tree when I was stuck by one of the long thorns that protruded out of the branches. To this day, I cannot understand why the branches of a lemon tree have such long, pointed thorns. In order to get to the lemons to make lemon juice, I had to get through the thorns. Many people want to drink lemonade, but how many of them would be willing to battle through the thorns to get the lemon to make the juice?

In the same manner that the citrus trees had to be pruned to increase the yield or the quality of the fruit, God the Husbandman has to prune the branches that are in the vine, which is Jesus. The pit is one of the places where the pruning process takes place. Jesus said, *"I am the true vine, and my Father is the husbandman. Every branch in me that beareth not fruit he taketh away: and every branch that beareth fruit, he purgeth it, that it may bring forth more fruit"* (John 15:1-2). Pruning is necessary in a tree for deadwood removal and shaping in order to control the growth and direction of the tree. God is a God of the living, and He is going to remove every dead thing from our lives in order to facilitate the direction in which He wants us to go. God has not called us out of darkness to have us wander aimlessly through life. The steps of a righteous man are ordered by the Lord. God has a divine destination for His children, and He has a plan to get them to their destination.

Arborists, orchardists, and gardeners use pruning shears, loppers, and chain saws to complete the pruning process. The type of tool used in pruning is determined by the tree or plant being pruned. The level of pruning in the life of the believer is determined by the level of revelation in which they operate, or the divine assignment God has chosen for them to fulfill. No gardener in his right mind would use a chain saw to prune a small rose bush, and a hand held clipper would not be the best tool to prune an oak tree. God knows the precise, specific tool necessary to achieve perfect pruning in the lives of His children. God desires vibrant, living branches on His vine because at some point, a dead branch will decay back to the parent stem, causing abscission and fall off, which can be dangerous. God has planted us in Jesus, and He will do whatever it takes to make sure we not only remain in Him but are also productive.

Joseph's assignment was in Egypt, but to get there, he had to go through the pit, Potiphar's house, and the prison. The palace was the place of his divine assignment, but he had to go through a process to get there. Concerning Jesus, the writer to the Hebrews said, *"Who for the joy that was set before him endured the cross, despising the shame, and is set down at the right hand of the throne of God"* (Hebrews 12:2b).

The Son of God had a position at the right hand of God, but to get there, He had to go through the cross. The Apostle Paul would write two-thirds of the New Testament and win many to Christ, but in defense of his apostleship to the people of Corinth, who questioned it, Paul wrote, *"Are they Hebrews? So am I. Are they Israelites? So am I. Are they the seed of Abraham? So am I. Are they ministers of Christ? (I speak as a fool) I am more: in labours more abundant, in stripes above measure, in prisons more frequent, in deaths oft. Of the Jews five times received I forty stripes save one. Thrice was I beaten with rods, once was I stoned, thrice I suffered shipwreck, a night and a day I have been in the deep; In journeyings often, in perils of waters, in perils of robbers, in perils by mine own countrymen, in perils by the heathen, in perils in the city, in perils in the wilderness, in perils in the sea, in perils among false brethren; In weariness and painfulness, in watching often, in hunger and thirst, in fastings often, in cold and nakedness. Beside those things that are without, that which cometh upon me daily, the care of all the churches" (2 Corinthians 11:25-28).* He does not list his qualifications as the amount of letters he wrote, or his title as apostle, or the fact that he studied at the feet of Gamaliel. He wants the reader to know the things that he had to suffer for the Gospel's sake. He had a great assignment in Christ, so he had to go through an arduous pruning process.

I am sure Joseph did not understand what was happening to him when his brothers attacked him, but he was able to survive the process because he had a word from the Lord. The same word from the Lord that gives us direction and instruction is the same word that will try us. You have the Word of the Lord in your belly, so don't be afraid to draw on it when you are in the pruning process. The pruning that takes place in the pit of your affliction or the prison of your present circumstance will prepare you for purpose. The greatest pruning tool in the life of the believer is the Word of God, and that is why His word is compared to a sword. *"For the word of God is quick, and powerful, and sharper than any two-edged sword, piercing even to the dividing asunder of soul and spirit, and of the joints and marrow, and is a discerner of the thoughts and intents of the heart" (Hebrews 4:12).*

The Word of God will divide or separate the things of the soul from the spirit. It will shine a light in the chambers of our hearts and reveal to us things that we have hidden deep below the surface. The Word of God is like a heat-seeking missile that never misses its target. His Word will always expose the thoughts and intents of our hearts. The question is whether or not we will be willing to handle what is revealed.

Just like Joseph, every believer has to go through the pruning process to get us ready to fulfill our divine assignment; there can and will be no exemptions. If we are to produce fruit for the Lord, then we have to yield to the process. Joseph had a great understanding of this concept and a great trust in God, and that is why you never hear complaints from him at any time in the process. There were no complaints in the pruning pit, no complaints in the pit of Potiphar's house, and no complaints in the pruning prison.

Pruning is an arboricultural practice involving the selective removal of parts of a plant. This practice usually entails removal of diseased, damaged, dead, non-productive, or otherwise unwanted tissue from a plant—such as branches, buds, or roots. Although the branch is bearing fruit, Jesus said His Father has to purge or prune it in order to get more fruit. He will not allow us to wallow in mediocrity; He desires maximum fruit production. The Greek word for purge is *kathairo* (pronounced *kath-ah-ee-roo*); it comes from a root word that means *to cleanse, to prune, or to expiate*. We have to be cleansed of all dead and putrefying flesh so our lives can yield the type of fruit that is pleasing to our Heavenly Father.

Have you ever been to the super market and bought some expensive grapes that you thought were sweet? They looked colorful and luscious to the eye, but when you tasted them you realized you were deceived by the looks. If you are a fruit lover, you know how nice it is to get a fruit that is ripe and sweet. On the other hand, you know how horrible it is when you get a fruit that is sour. When the devil is in control of a person's life, their fruit is sour, but when they allow Jesus to come in, God will prune the person so the fruit will be sweet. You don't have to guess what type of spirit a person is operating in—just do a fruit check. Jesus said, *"Beware of false prophets, which come to you in sheep's clothing, but inwardly they are ravening wolves. You shall know them by their fruits. Do men gather grapes of thorns, or figs of thistles? Even so every good tree bringeth forth good fruit; but a corrupt tree bringeth forth evil fruit. A good tree cannot bring forth evil fruit, neither can a corrupt tree bring forth good fruit. Every tree that bringeth not forth good fruit is hewn down, and cast into the fire. Wherefore by their fruits ye shall know them" (Matthew 7:17-20).*

In his letter to the Galatians, Paul lists the fruit of the Spirit as love, joy, peace, longsuffering, gentleness, goodness, faith, meekness, and temperance. If a person is not manifesting any of the aforementioned fruits, then you know they are operating from a different spirit from the Holy Spirit. The Holy Spirit bears fruit in the life of the believer, but the flesh manifests works, and they are adultery, fornication, uncleanness, lasciviousness, idolatry, witchcraft, hatred, variance, emulations, wrath, strife, seditions, heresies, envy, murder, drunkenness, and revellings. God uses the pit and the pruning process to burn out the works of the flesh so the fruit of the Spirit can be developed in us.

Jesus said, *"Now ye are clean through the word which I have spoken unto you. Abide in me, and I in you. As the branch cannot bear fruit of itself, except it abide in the vine; no more can ye, except ye abide in me. I am the vine, ye are the branches: He that abideth in me, and I in him, the same bringeth forth much fruit: for without me ye can do nothing" (John 15: 1-2).* Please notice the progression described by Jesus in John 15. The end result of the pruning process is to produce **fruit**, **more fruit**, and then **much fruit**. It is a threefold process in the life of the child of Christ. The number three is symbolic of resurrection, divine completeness, and perfect testimony. One plants, one waters, but at the third stage God gives the increase. All of us have a beginning, middle, and an end. In the beginning of our walk with Christ, we start to bear fruit, and as we progress in Him, we bear more fruit as the Father prunes us; then we get to the stage of perfection where our life bears much fruit. You can see these stages in the life of Joseph as he goes from the pit, to Potiphar's house, to the prison. These three phases of his life prepared him to bear much fruit in the palace.

In order for maximum production to take place, the believer or the branch must abide in Jesus, the vine. The Greek word for abide is *meno* (pronounced *men-o*). It is a primary verb that means *to stay in a given place, state, relation, or expectancy.* Some Christians are not bearing fruit because they will not stay in a local church long enough for the word to try, prune, and cleanse them. They will not stay long in a marriage until death do us part. They will not stay long in school to get qualified for a job. They will not stay long in a business to reap the profits. It is said, "A rolling stone gathers no moss." No one plants a seed in the ground only to dig it up days later to see if it is starting to germinate. It has to stay in the ground long enough to be impacted by the soil, the sun, and the rain. Once the root starts to grow, it can be transplanted in different soil, but you will never have growth if you do not allow the seed to stay in the soil for the duration of time necessary. You cannot run from the designated place in which the Lord has placed you because there are some thorns in your flesh. Some of the biggest thorns you will encounter will be right in the Church, but you have to be willing to persevere. There is a reason why the Lord instructed us to let the wheat and the tare grow together. He knows how to deal with the tare so that the wheat does not sustain damage.

When Joseph was in the pruning pit of prison because of the false accusation of molestation from Potiphar's wife, he interpreted the dreams of a butler and a baker and asked the baker to remember him. *"But think on me when it shall be well with thee, and shew kindness, I pray thee, unto me, and make mention of me unto Pharaoh, and bring me out of this house: For indeed I was stolen away out of the land of the Hebrews: and here also have I done nothing that they should put me into the dungeon" (Genesis 40:14-154).* Have you ever showed kindness to someone by helping them out of a situation, and instead of being a blessing to you, when their breakthrough came they just went about their business? That is what Joseph experienced, but I believe God would not allow the butler to remember him because his season for release had not come. There is no timing like God's timing, and He saw fit to leave Joseph there after the butler was released because He knew there were some more things He had to do in and with Joseph. Man's actions do not control our blessings. God is in control. If you are in a pruning process right now, please don't be discouraged because the season of promotion is on the way, and God will not allow you to be there one minute longer than necessary. He wants to make sure once you are released that you will be able to handle the challenges that accompany promotion. Don't allow the people who have forsaken you to cause you stress.

You might have been abandoned by a wife or a husband. You might have been abandoned by a parent, or you might be a parent that has been abandoned by your children. Release them and ask God to bless them; make sure there is no unforgiveness in your heart. People can and will forget you, but the Lord will never forget you. He will never leave you nor forsake you.

Moses spent forty years in Egypt in the palace of Pharaoh as a prince, but in order to be prepared to lead a rebellious people, he had to spend forty years in the desert as a shepherd. The forty in the desert was preparation to lead God's people for forty years in the wilderness. After being baptized by John, the Spirit led Jesus into the desert to fast for forty days and forty nights so He could deal with the temptation of the devil. The Israelites traveled for forty years in the wilderness so God could prepare them to enter the Promised Land. Forty is the number of testing and probation. Every believer will have to endure times of testing and probation before they enter their season of promotion. *"To everything there is a season, and a time to every purpose under the heaven. A time to be born, and a time to die, a time to plant, and a time to pluck up that which is planted"* *(Ecclesiastes 3:1-2).*

You may be in a winter season, but hold on because spring is coming. If you are in the spring or summer season, then you should prepare because fall and winter are coming.

Joseph had to abide in the prison until his season of release came. Jesus said, *"If a man abide not in me, he is cast forth as a branch, and is withered; and men gather them, and cast them into the fire, and they are burned. If ye abide in me and my words abide in you ye shall ask what ye will, and it shall be done unto you. Herein is my Father glorified, that ye bear much fruit; so shall ye be my disciples"* (John 15: 6-8). If we are not willing to abide in the vine, we will wither. One of the reasons the branches of a tree die is light deficiency. A believer will not survive and thrive if he is not receiving a steady stream of light from the Son. Jesus said, *"I am the light of the world: he that followeth me shall not walk in darkness, but shall have the light of life"* *(John 8:12).* Plants need natural sunlight to grow, and believers need the light of the Son to grow. The Psalmist said, *"The entrance of thy word giveth light; it giveth understanding unto the simple. I opened my mouth and panted; for I longed for thy commandments" (Psalm 119:130).* The Psalmist needed the Word of God like a man dying of thirst needs water.

I cannot stress enough the importance of abiding in the place in which the Lord has planted us. Concerning the blessed man, Psalm 1 declares, *"Blessed is the man that walketh not in the counsel of the ungodly, nor standeth in the way of sinners, nor sitteth in the seat of the scornful. But his delight is inn the law of the Lord; and in his law doth he meditate day and night."* How often are you reading and meditating on the Word of God? I know there are times when I am going through a night or winter season when I struggle to read the Word of God and pray. Those are the times when I get my greatest breakthroughs—when I learn to press through those difficult seasons. Remember, the first word in breakthrough is *break.*

We will not experience God's best if we forsake the word and spend untold hours feeding our carnal nature with worldly things. God is glorified when we bear much fruit, but we can't get to the place of much fruit without the pruning process. Jesus actually ties our discipleship to our fruit production. Disciples don't run from the process because they realize that, although the process is not easy, it is through the process that God gets glory and much fruit out of us. The Apostle Paul asked the Lord to remove the thorn from his flesh, but the Lord responded by saying that His grace was sufficient for Paul because His strength was made perfect in Paul's weakness. Once Paul realized the Lord was perfecting strength in his weakness, he took his eyes off the weakness and said he would rather glory in his infirmities so the power of the Lord would rest upon him. It is better to go into the fire of purification than to bow to idols. Are you praying for the Lord to take you out of a situation that He is using to perfect His strength in you? Remember the three Hebrew boys. They told King Nebuchadnezzar that God was able to deliver them, but if He did not they still would not bow. This is the posture and the attitude the child of God has to adopt. We know God can deliver, but if He does not, then keep praising Him anyway, and know that He will be in the fire with you. When He is in the fire, the fire will not consume you—it will purify you.

Out of the Pit—Into the Palace

The brash Joseph who told his brothers and his father they would do obeisance to him was not the same Joseph who would stand before Pharaoh. Once his time came, the Lord allowed Pharaoh to dream a dream that could not be interpreted by any of the wise men in Egypt. How awesome is it that the wise men of Egypt could not interpret the dream, but a Hebrew slave dwelling in Pharaoh's dungeon for something he did not do, was the one with the interpretation. You might be enduring the pruning process of a pit or a dungeon right now, but God is already setting in motion the events that will lead to your release. When He brings you out, you will have a testimony that will help deliver others. Once He delivers you, He wants to make sure that when you get to the palace and He uses you, He will get all the Glory. When Joseph spoke to his brothers and father, he didn't give God the Glory: *"And he said unto them, Hear, I pray you, this dream which I have dreamed" (Genesis 37: 6).* It was all about "I," and there was no mention of God—probably because at seventeen, there was not a great deal of maturity. He had it pretty good at that time because of his status as his father's favorite. Favoritism can spoil a child if it is excessive. The child can go from feeling special to feeling entitled. I am sure Joseph enjoyed his position as the favorite, and I am also sure he was excited about the dream.

He did not know when he told them about the dream that it would contain a nightmare called the pit, Potiphar's house, and the prison. It is all about enduring the process of your promotion. Anyone can shout when the battle is over and they are victorious. Anyone can shout when the struggle is over, but can you shout in the pit? Can you shout in the midst of the accusations? Can you shout Hallelujah in the prison?

I have a radical praise because I remember the days when I praised Him in the pig pen. The pruning process of the pit, the pig pen, and the prison will teach you how to praise Him. It will burn false pride out of you and teach you that you are nothing without Jesus. I blasphemed the name of Jesus when I was on the streets indulging in crime, but I had to bow my knee and give Him the Glory when I was in the prison cell.

I love what Paul told the Philippians. He said, *"Let this mind be in you which was also in Christ Jesus: Who, being in the form of God, thought it not robbery to be equal with God: But made himself of no reputation, and took upon him the form of a servant, and was made in the likeness of men: And being found in fashion as a man, he humbled himself, and became obedient unto death, even the death of the cross. Wherefore God has highly exalted him, and given him a name which is above every name. That at the name of Jesus every knee should bow, of things in heaven and things in earth, and things under the earth; and that every tongue should confess that Jesus Christ is Lord, to the glory of God the Father"* (Philippians (2: 5-11).

Far too many people in the body of Christ are trying to make a name for themselves as the next great prophet, preacher, or psalmist. Joseph had a reputation as the favorite, but God is not interested in our reputation; He is interested in our consecration. Joseph was thrown into the pit by his brothers, sold into slavery by traders, tried in the fire by enduring the lies of Potiphar's wife; he was forgotten about by the chief butler after interpreting his dream, but God never forgot Joseph, and God has not forgotten you. God prospered him in the process. Your process might be difficult to endure, but if you allow Him to, God will prosper you in the midst of it. The Lord was with Joseph and prospered him in Potiphar's house. Potiphar could see that the Hand of the Lord was on Joseph's life. He was promoted to overseer of the house, and Potiphar's house was blessed by the Lord because Joseph was there. Keep in mind the fact that Joseph was still a slave in Egypt, but he was on a course of divine destiny.

The favor of God did not stop when Joseph was the victim of a lie that caused him to be put in prison. The LORD was with him in prison and gave him favor in the sight of the keeper of the prison. Joseph was put in charge of all the prisoners. When you are a child of God, and you are willing to yield to the pruning process, God will elevate you in whatever place He plants you. The years I spent in prison turned out to be a blessing for me because I yielded to Jesus, and He used me to be a blessing to other inmates.

The Bible declares, "And *it came to pass at the end of two full years, that Pharaoh dreamed"* (Genesis 40:41a). Notice the use of the word "full." He would not be released a moment before the time ordained by God. Isn't it amazing that it was a dream that started Joseph's pruning process from the pit to Potiphar's house, then to the prison, and it is a dream that allowed him to be brought to the palace, the place of his divine assignment, to give Pharaoh the interpretation of his dream? God allowed the baker to tell Pharaoh about the young Hebrew in the dungeon who interpreted his dream, so Pharaoh sent for Joseph. The Apostle Paul said, *"For I reckon that the sufferings of this present time are not worthy to be compared with the glory which shall be revealed in us" (Romans 8:8).* Dr. Samuel Greene always tells us that "suffering is tied to the Glory." The Greek word for Glory is *doxa* (pronounced *dox-ah*), and it means *honour, dignity, praise, and worship.* The Hebrew word for Glory is *kabowd* (pronounced *kaw-bode*), and it means *weight, splendor, and honor.* Joseph had gone through the process, and now he was in the palace—the place of divine purpose.

You can't get to the palace or the pinnacle unless you are willing to be pruned in the pit. Joseph was brought hastily out of the dungeon. Your time in the pit and the pruning process might seem extraordinarily long, but when your season of deliverance comes, it will come expeditiously.

Joseph stood before the most powerful leader at that time, and the Word of the Lord was about to manifest in his life. He was tried by the Word, but now the manifestation of the words he'd spoken to his family was coming to pass—only this time, God would get the Glory. The *Apostle* Paul declared, *"I am crucified with Christ: nevertheless I live; yet not I, but Christ liveth in me: and the life which I now live in the flesh I live by the faith of the Son of God, who loved me, and gave himself for me" (Galatians 2:20).* Jesus gave His life for us when we were trapped in sin and trespass, so we can only imagine how much He will give to us now that we are in a covenant relationship with Him. We have to die to the flesh daily so He can mature us.

John the Baptist said, *"I must decrease so he can increase."* It is imperative that we decrease if we expect the Holy Ghost to increase in us. The Holy Ghost will not dwell in a vessel where flesh is allowed to increase. The death of the flesh and the growth in Joseph's life is evident in his response to Pharaoh's dream. The "I" spoken to his brothers and his father has died in the pruning process, and now he responds to Pharaoh's dream by saying, *"It is not in me: God shall give Pharaoh an answer of peace" Genesis 41:16). Hallelujah!!!* What an awesome transformation. Joseph knew that the answer Pharaoh needed was not in his human ability. God had the answer of peace Pharaoh needed. The pruning process will get flesh out of the way so God can use us to speak peace to someone's turbulent situation.

Once Joseph gave the interpretation of the dream to Pharaoh, The Bible says, *"And the thing was good in the eyes of Pharaoh, and in the eyes of all his servants" (Genesis 41:37).* It was not Pharaoh alone who witnessed the gift God had perfected in Joseph. His appearing was evident to all. Many of the trials we have endured were evident for people to see, and when God brings out our deliverance, it will be evident to many, even those who were not supportive of us in the storm. Joseph was a gifted young man but to get glory out of his gifts, he had to endure the pruning process of the pit, the lies of Potiphar's wife, and the prison.

"A man's gift maketh room for him, and bringeth him before great men" (Proverbs 18:16). I always thought the word gift in that verse meant some ability to preach, teach, or sing that opened doors to greatness for an individual, but how wrong I was. The Hebrew word for gift is *mattan* (pronounced *mat-tawn*), and it means *a present, to give, or to reward.* It is the things you are willing to give or give up that will open the door for you so that you may stand before great men. Joseph had to give up the life he lived with his family as the favorite son to become a slave, but it was what he gave up that opened the door for him to stand before a great man like Pharaoh. Jesus gave up the riches of heaven to come to earth as a suffering servant, but it was that gift that opened the door for us to stand before Him, the great God-Man. Hallelujah!!!

"And Pharaoh said unto his servants, can we find such a one as this is, a man in whom the spirit of God is? And Pharaoh said unto Joseph, forasmuch as God hath shewed thee all this; there is none so discreet and wise as thou art" (Genesis 41: 38-39). Dr. Samuel Greene said that God is not looking for a superman. God is not looking for a man, woman, or child with ability. He is looking for *availability.* I believe the greatest thing that can be said of a man is not how smart or how rich he is; the greatest thing that can be said about him is, *the Spirit of God is in him.*

When a man is willing to die to ambition and pride, when he is willing to die to the lust of the eyes, the lust of the flesh, and the pride of life, the Spirit of God will take up residence within him.

At the age of seventeen, when Joseph spoke to his brothers and his father, he was not very discreet, but it is evident that Joseph has learned great wisdom from the trials he had to endure. Remember, Moses said one of the purposes of the wilderness is to humble the people of God. Do not fight the Holy Ghost fire; just yield to the process, and you will not get burned. The fire is sent to purify, not to scorch.

Random House *Webster's Collegiate Dictionary* defines the word discreet as, *"judicious in ones conduct or speech, especially with regard to keeping silent about a delicate matter."* The word as it is used in English can have the connotation of hiding or keeping something secret. The Hebrew for discreet is *biyn* (pronounced *bene);* it means *to separate mentally or to distinguish.* It also means *to be prudent, to think, to have intelligence, or to teach.* Pharaoh and the men around him were able to witness the Spirit of Wisdom from Joseph.

Pharaoh set Joseph over his house and over all the land of Egypt. Beloved, can you see the progression from fruit to more fruit, and finally, to much fruit in the life of Joseph? He was the most powerful man in Egypt next to Pharaoh. The race is not given to the swift neither to the strong, but to those who can endure. Our process is one of endurance. If we are able to hold on to the unchanging hand of the Master, He will promote us in due season. It is absolutely amazing how Joseph came to Egypt as a slave but is now elevated to second in command; it shows that with God, all things are possible and His words concerning our lives will not return to him empty or void. God's Word will accomplish His purpose for your life, so trust in His Word, believe His report, and know that every contrary word is a lie from the devil.

God's word will come to pass in your life, and He will move heaven and earth to bring it to pass if He has to. What you are going through is nothing but a test, and the beauty of it is that it is an open book test. The Bible has all the answers, so apply them to the test. A test is given to see how well you have learned your lesson. Your test is designed for you and no one else. Your test will always be commensurate to your divine assignment from the Lord. Pharaoh put a ring on Joseph's finger, and the ring is symbolic of authority and power in another's name. He was standing in Pharaoh's authority, but it was God who was pulling the strings. He arrayed Joseph in vestures of fine linen, which is symbolic of moral purity and righteousness. His brothers stripped him of the coat of many colors given to him by his father, but now he has vestures given to him by Pharaoh, King of Egypt. The things the enemy has stripped from you will be replaced by something greater so do not fret, just keep trusting in God.

There is great revelation concerning the changing or the putting on of an individual's garment in the scriptures. When the Amalekites burned Ziklag with fire and took David's wives and the wives and children of all his men, David sent for the ephod. The ephod was a sacred vestment worn originally by the high priest and later by ordinary priests. It was characteristic of the priest's office. It was made of fine linen and consisted of two pieces, which hung from the neck and covered both the back and front above the tunic and outer garment. The garment of the high priest was embroidered with diverse colors. Remember, Joseph's father gave him a coat of many colors, and that is what his brothers stripped him of. The soldiers cast lots for the garment of Jesus. The breastplate, with the Urim and Thummim, was attached to the ephod. The priest put on the garment when they inquired of the Lord.

We have the garment of praise, and it is like fine linen; it is like the ephod. When we put on the garment of praise and take off the spirit of heaviness, we can pursue, overtake, and recover all.

"And David inquired at the Lord, saying, Shall I pursue after this troop? Shall I overtake them? And he answered him, Pursue: for thou shalt surely overtake them, and without fail recover all" (1 Samuel 30:8).

Pharaoh put a gold chain on Joseph's neck. Gold is symbolic of kingship, kingdom of glory, and God or gods. Now the people of Egypt had to bow to Joseph as a god. Jesus told the Pharisees, *"Is it not written in your law, I said, ye are gods?" (John 10:34).*

Remember, Joseph was thirty years old when he stood before Pharaoh, and thirty is the number that is symbolic of consecration and maturity for ministry. Thirteen years had passed since seventeen-year-old Joseph told his dream to his brethren. Thirteen is the number of rebellion, and it took thirteen long years for Joseph to get to the place of exercising wisdom and discretion.

Further proof of Joseph's maturity is seen when he encounters his brothers after many years and much affliction. A famine forced his brothers to come to Egypt to buy corn. *"And Joseph was the governor over the land, and he it was that sold to all the people of the land: and Joseph's brethren came, and bowed down themselves before him with their faces to the earth" (Genesis 42:6).* His dream of his brothers bowing before him had now come to pass. He would not have been able to handle that at seventeen, but now there was a greater maturity level gained from the pruning process in the pit, in Potiphar's house, and in the prison. Joseph recognized his brothers, but they did not recognize him. It is evident there was not much transformation in the lives of his brothers because Joseph was able to recognize them after many years. Joseph's life was totally transformed, and his brothers could not recognize him. He looked much better now than when they'd last seen him because God restored him, and when God restores you, your latter days will be greater than your former. Remember how God restored Job after the pit of sickness and the loss of his livestock and his children? *"So the Lord blessed the latter end of Job more than his beginning: for he had fourteen thousand sheep, and six thousand camels, and a thousand yoke of oxen, and a thousand she asses. He had also seven sons and three daughters. And he called the name of the first, Jemima; and the name of the second Kezia; and the name of the third, Keren-happuch. And in all the land were no women found so fair as the daughters of Job: and their father gave them inheritance among their brethren. After this lived Job an hundred and forty years, and saw his sons, and his sons' sons, even four generations. So Job died, being old and full of days" (Job 42: 12-17).*

Seven and three are both symbolic of Divine perfection and completion. There was no sibling rivalry here because the daughters of Job received their inheritance along with their brothers.

When Joseph revealed his identity to his brothers, he was not full of anger and had no desire for revenge. He was mature enough to know that God had allowed them to afflict him for a purpose. He told them that God had sent him before them to preserve life. Do not allow your anger and bitterness towards your ex-spouse, boss, pastor, or friend to cloud your mind and cause you to miss what God has done in terms of giving you a ministry out of that misery.

God's ways are not our ways, and his thoughts are not our thoughts. We see through a glass dimly lit, but God has a panoramic view, which means He sees the ending from the beginning. The ending was for Joseph to preserve life not only for his brothers but also for the Egyptians and the people of the surrounding nations. At the present time, we might not be able to fully comprehend the fullness of God's plan for our lives, and we might have a difficult time trying to process the pruning we are experiencing, but God knows the ending from the beginning, and we must place our complete trust and confidence in Him. If we adopt the right posture and attitude in the time of trial, we will experience promotion at every level of the process, just as Joseph did. He was promoted in Potiphar's house, he was promoted in the prison, and he was promoted when he stood before Pharaoh in the palace. I am sure there were many days when Joseph longed to be back with his family, even the brothers that betrayed him.

When you are away from home, away from your loved ones, there will always be a longing. I think of all the inmates that are separated from their loved ones without a visit for years. During my time away from my family, I was kept strong by keeping my mind on the Word of God and not on the things or the people I missed. If you are reading this from a prison cell or a place that has you separated from your wife, kids, or other loved ones, please be patient. It is difficult for you to see the end of the process right now, but God knows the outcome, and it is better to trust Him. Find a place of peace in the pruning process and just give Him some praise. Praise shows God that you are mature enough to trust Him even though your deliverance has not come. God inhabits the praises of His people, and praise will bring Him into your sphere.

Joseph did not quit serving God when his brothers betrayed him and threw him in the pit; he did not quit when he was sold into Egypt as a slave; he did not quit when Potiphar's wife lied, and he did not quit when it was evident that the butler forgot about him. Wherever he found himself, he behaved wisely, and I believe that is the reason why he was promoted in every phase of the pruning process. Do not think about quitting. Rebuke the spirit of suicide the devil is trying to put in your mind. Cry out to the Lord and ask Him to help you to make it through this season. If you call, He will answer. Do not drown your sorrows in alcohol, drugs, or sexual perversion. Dig your heels in and fight the good fight of faith.

It is easy to become bitter and disillusioned over the things you are facing, and God knows your struggle is not easy. He is strengthening and fortifying you for the work He has called you to do. Draw strength from the people like Joseph, David, Moses, Esther, and from Jesus. He is the Author and the Finisher of your Faith, but your faith has to be tried in the fire. If anyone had a right to quit it would have been Jesus. Can you imagine being beaten, spat upon, and nailed to a cross to redeem guilty people from death and destruction? Remember, the writer in the book of Hebrews said, "He endured the cross and despised the shame." The writer also reminds us that we "have not resisted unto blood." In the **Garden of Gethsemane,** Jesus agonized while His disciples slept; Jesus asked His Father to take the cup if it were possible, but I like the fact that He said, *"nevertheless not my will but thine be done."* You are going through your dealings for what God is trying to do in and through you, but Jesus' dealings were for the whole human race. When the battle gets tough, just say, "Lord, not my will but thine be done."

My maternal grandmother's favorite song was "I come to the garden alone." When I think of a garden, I get thoughts of a beautiful place where flowers are grown, but the phrase "Garden of Gethsemane" seems like a paradox because Gethsemane means oil press, and that particular garden was the scene of Jesus' agony. We cannot get the oil unless the olive is crushed. The cross was not the first place where Jesus shed blood—the Garden of Gethsemane was. He endured a crushing in the garden until His sweat was drops of blood.

There are many of us who are dealing with what I call self-inflicted wounds. Many of us are dealing with the repercussions of choices that we made in the flesh. The law of action and reaction, cause and effect, dictates that what a man sows is what he will reap. God's mercy does not allow us to have to take the full penalty because without His Mercy, our sins would kill us. We like to see transgressors punished to the max, but I thank God that His judgment is just and righteous. If we examine our lives, we can honestly say that if God gave us what we deserved for the things we did in the flesh, we would have been cut off a long time ago. Someone said He is a God of a second chance, but I know Him as a God of third and fourth chances because I used up my second chance a long time ago!

The drops of blood Jesus sweated and the cross He endured was for the purpose of delivering us from the penalty of our sinful nature. He was crushed so we would not be crushed by the sin in our lives. God understands our weaknesses and frailties, and that is why He is patient with us. Although He is long suffering, we will suffer long if we do not flee worldliness and learn the things He is teaching us through our trials. Once you realize that you have lived a life that was not pleasing to God, why not make a decision to walk upright before Him? Why not surrender to Him and allow Him to do great things with you while you are alive? It is not easy to take a stand for God in a world that is becoming darker and more sinful, but God expects His children to stand for righteousness and cry out to Him for those who are trapped in bondage. Sin has terrible consequences and can lead to death if there is no repentance. I learned first-hand of the death and destruction sin can cause when I was put in a place where I was forced to examine the wickedness of my heart. I didn't like what I saw. I saw a heart that was consumed by sin, and I saw a life that was on the brink of destruction.

CHAPTER 3

The Pit of Sin

**"For all have sinned, and come short of
the glory of God" (Romans 3:23).**

Sin

Sin is a three letter word, but its consequences are grave. Random House *Webster's Collegiate Dictionary* defines sin as a transgression of divine law; a willful violation of some religious or moral principle. Louis Sperry Chafer writes in *Systematic Theology* that sin "is essentially a restlessness unwillingness on the part of the creature to abide in the sphere and limitation in which the all-wise Creator placed him. In general, sin is the lack of conformity to the character of God." (Systematic theology, ed. By John F. Walvoord {2vols; Wheaton: Victor Books, 1988}, I, 367.)

Sin simply means missing the mark of perfection established by God. Think of an archer shooting his arrows at his target hoping to get a bull's-eye but missing miserably every time. We all miss the mark at one time or another because without Jesus Christ, we continue to fall short of God's perfect standard or His standard of perfection. It is probably easy for an individual to feel because he is not a murderer, a drug dealer, a rapist or the perpetrator of some heinous act that he is exempted from the classification of a sinner, but no one gets a free pass when it comes to sin. *"All have sinned and come short of the glory of God" (Romans 3:23).* The Bible states it clearly and emphatically.

All means all, and all means everyone. According to the Bible commentary, Paul explained that "no difference" existed among human beings because all have sinned. The Greek is literally, "all sinned" (*pantes hemarton*). The entire human race was plunged into sin with Adam.

Not only did all sin, but all fell short. This single Greek verb is in the present tense, stressing continuing action. It can be translated to mean "keep on falling short." The simple fact is that as a sinner, not a single human being by his own efforts is able to measure up to the Glory of God. God's glory is His splendor, the outward manifestation of His attributes. God desires that humans share that splendor, that they become like Him; that is, Christ-like, yet their sins keep them from sharing it.

There isn't a person in this world who has the right to look at someone else through self-righteous, judgmental eyes because the other person committed some terrible sin. I believe we, as Christians, have a tendency to forget from where the Lord brought us. I heard a precious sister in the Lord say we are all a bunch of "ex's"—the sin the Blood of Jesus washed us from is what the ex represents. Some of us are ex-whoremongers, adulterers, drunkards, and liars. God does not allow any of us to take solace in self-righteousness. He uses the strongest of terms to describe man's futile attempt at righteousness. *"But we are all as an unclean thing, and all our righteousness are as filthy rags; and we all do fade as a leaf; and our iniquities, like the wind, have taken us away."* In Hebrew, Isaiah 64:6 is much more graphic in its description than in the King James version. In Hebrew it says, "All our righteousness is as the rag of a menstruous woman."

Sin is not something that should be glossed over or spoken of in euphemistic terms because it grieves the Heart of God. In speaking to the children of Israel, God said, *"But your iniquities have separated between you and your God, and your sins have hid his face from you, that he will not hear"* (Isaiah 59:2). What could be worse than being separated from God? There are people who are deceived into thinking God is hearing and answering their prayers although they have not surrendered to the Lordship of Jesus. The Bible clearly states that the sun shines on the just and the unjust, and the prayer God desires to hear from a sinner is the prayer of repentance. I am convinced the devil will allow people to receive certain things in order to keep them in a place of self-deception where they think the Lord is blessing them, so it is okay for them to continue living life without Jesus.

When you compare the pleasures of sin for a season and its consequences with the joy and the refreshment that comes from the presence of God, you come to the realization that no pleasure from sin can be compared to the joy of abiding in His presence. How many times have you heard someone who is not in a covenant relationship with God say, "God is answering my prayers," or "God is blessing me"? These statements go against what the Bible teaches and is proof that there is a spirit of deception in operation. Jesus spoke of the broad way that leads to death, upon which many people travel, and the narrow way, which leads to eternal life. Isaiah clearly stated that sins cause God's face to be hidden from His people, and when His face is hidden, He does not hear their prayers. It might appear that the sinner is enjoying the blessings of God through answered prayers, but they are not. If a person can get answers to prayers and remain in the presence of God despite their sins, then why would there be any need to repent?

God's mercy ensures that we don't always get punished as soon as we sin, but the lack of instant punishment does not mean God is pleased with us despite our sins. God gives us the opportunity to repent or turn from our sins for the sole purpose of keeping us from destruction and allowing us to return to His presence. While He takes no delight in the death of the wicked, His righteousness does demand that sinners be judged.

It would be silly to classify every sin in the same category because the Bible talks about the sin that leads to death, so by reason of deduction, there are probably sins that don't lead to death. I might be presumptuous in saying this, but I believe God looks at the individual that steals a loaf of bread to feed his family in a different light than he looks at the person who has an abundance but steals out of greed. It is not just a matter of the things we do and the things we don't do. It is a matter of the unregenerate sin nature that will lead us into acts that break God's moral code.

The Journey

Sin will take you farther than you want to go. It will keep you longer than you want to stay. It will cost you more than you want to pay. *"For the wages of sin is death; but the gift of God is eternal life through Jesus Christ our Lord."* Sin will land you in a pit and keep you from getting to the palace. Sin does pay, but the price it pays is not the price we want to earn because no one in their right mind desires death as their wage. Sin leads us all on a journey that ultimately leads to death, unless Jesus Christ intervenes. Webster's dictionary defines death as "a permanent cessation of all vital functions: the end of life." Although death is often associated with extinction, in the Bible it never means the end of existence. Biblically, death means separation from or the inability to function in a particular realm.

In his book, *The Basics* (A Categorical Bible Study), Gene Cunningham describes the seven deaths described in the Word of God. **Spiritual death** is a separation from God. As a result of the fall, all human beings are born spiritually dead, captives of *"the domain of darkness" (Gen. 2:17; Col. 1:13; Rom. 6:23).*

Positional death is separation from sin and the sin nature. Every believer is made spiritually alive and placed in Christ at salvation. We now have the ability to choose every moment whether we will serve our old sin nature, or our new nature (Rom. 6: 1-4, 10-11; Gal. 2:20; Col. 2:12, 20, 3:3).

Temporal death is carnality, separation from fellowship with God. Every time we, as Christians, give in to temptation to sin, we enter temporal death (James 1:15 Rom. 8:2, 6, 13; 1 Tim. 5:6).

Operational death is separation of our profession of faith from the practice of that faith (James 2:26; Eph. 5:14; 1 John 1:5-6).

Sexual death is the inability to function sexually (Rom. 4: 19-20; Heb. 11:11-12).

Physical death is the separation of soul and body, the inability to function in the physical realm (Heb. 9:27; Gen. 5:5).

The second death is the judgment of unbelievers, eternal separation from God (Rev. 19-20).

With that said, why do we sin if death is the payment or the wage? We sin because sin is pleasurable, and we don't think about the consequences or the penalty. We sin because there are areas in our lives that we have not surrendered to Jesus. We sin because without Jesus, we are under the control of the sin nature. The Apostle Paul summed up the struggle within beautifully in his letter to the Church at Rome.

"For I know that in me (that is, in my flesh,) dwelleth no good thing: for to will is present with me; but how to perform that which is good I find not. For the good that I would I do not: but the evil which I would not, that I do. Now if I do that I would not, it is no more I that do it, but sin that dwelleth in me. I find then a law, that, when I would do good, evil is present with me. For I delight in the law of God after the inward man: But I see another law in my members, warring against the law of my mind, and bringing me into captivity to the law of sin which is in my members. O wretched man that I am! who shall deliver me from the body of this death? I thank God through Jesus Christ our Lord. So then with the mind I myself serve the law of God; but with the flesh the law of sin" (Romans 7:18-25).

If a devotee of Christ like the Apostle Paul can honestly say that he had a struggle with sin, then what is the condition of the person who has not surrendered to Jesus? That person has to be under the total control of their carnal, sinful nature. A person can be raised up and taught the difference between right and wrong, but if the root of sin, which is in the person's nature, is not dealt with, that individual will be overpowered at various points in life by that sin nature. There is no one, no matter how moral he or she may be, who can withstand the repeated onslaught and the bombarding on the mind by sinful thoughts. We might be able to resist certain things, but everyone has a weakness to something. If a Christian has to die daily in terms of resisting sin, then the sinner does not stand a chance of overcoming his or her desire or appetite for sin without the power of Jesus in their life.

The sinful journey is one we probably would not take if we knew the price we would pay. Hindsight is twenty-twenty, so when we look back over our lives, we can see the correlation between the things we suffered and the sinful acts that led to the suffering.

The journey of a thousand miles begins with the first step. For all of us, the journey of this life began at conception and the subsequent entrance into our mother's womb and ends when we take our last breath. Life's journey is not over when we take our last breath—only our journey in these mortal bodies. The life we live is determined by how we are brought up and the type of family of which we are a part. We are birthed into a world riddled and racked with sin, and that sin impacts our lives and the decisions we make.

I believe there is a correlation between our family lineage and the types of sin with which we struggle. Children who are born into families that struggle with sexual perversion will be susceptible to spirits of perversion. Children born into families with chronic alcohol and drug abuse will face struggles in that area. We are products of our environment, and when the desire in our sin nature connects or is stimulated by something in the world, we will be enticed into some type of sinful act. An individual might have an inner desire for sexual perversion upon which he does not act, but if he opens the door to pornography, he will eventually act upon his desires. The pornography will trigger something is his soul where the desire for sexual perversion is laying dormant, waiting for an opportunity to manifest.

Sin was passed down to all human beings through Adam, so sin affects all of Adam's descendants. There are some people who do not believe in original sin, but I believe in the same manner that there are things passed on to us from our parents and their parents through our genes and our bloodline; so sin was passed on to all humans through Adam. It does not matter if you are rich or poor, black or white. If you are a human being, you will struggle with some form of sin. I know it is common when sin is mentioned to think of certain types of sin, but remember, pride can be a type of sin, unforgiveness another type, and covetousness, or gluttony another type. It is easy to point the finger at someone trapped in homosexuality, pornography, or adultery, but how about the Christian who is unwilling to forgive his brother? How about the Christian who closes off his well of compassion when he sees a brother or sister with a need?

Our adversary, the devil, is a master illusionist, so he entices us on this journey of sin with things that are pleasing to the flesh but bitter to the soul. His desire is to get us to taste the forbidden thing in hopes of getting us hooked. Once we are hooked, then the journey of death begins because we will continue to partake of it until we are delivered or it destroys us. When you think of individuals like politicians or priests whose lives and careers were destroyed because of sexual impropriety, you realize that a seed was planted somewhere along the way, and because it was not dealt with, it grew until it bore fruit—but not the good kind of fruit. When you hear stories of a president being caught in a situation where he had oral sex with an intern in the white house, or a presidential candidate who gets his mistress pregnant while his wife is battling with breast cancer—then you know the devil is involved. What about the preacher of a large congregation who gets exposed by his gay, drug supplying masseuse? When the masseuse hears him pontificate about the evils of homosexuality in one of his televised sermons, he winds up exposing their tryst on national television. People that live in glass houses should not throw stones or carry bones. It is easy to wave a judgmental finger and say, how could that person do such a thing? There is a certain thrill and an adrenaline rush to partaking of the forbidden fruit, but that fruit is bitter to the stomach once the individual is caught. Both the individual and their family have to live with the shame and the degradation when their sexual tryst or some other moral transgression becomes public news.

Sexual sins have to be some of the hardest to deal with. Please understand that all sin is impossible to deal with without first being washed in the Blood of Jesus and yielded to the power of the Holy Ghost. The Bible gives us clear warning of the pit of sexual sin.

The Bible warns us to flee from youthful lusts. I will share a couple of examples of places in the scripture where it warns young people and people in general of the danger of illicit relationships and sex outside of the confines of marriage. *"My son, keep my words, and lay up my commandments with thee. Keep my commandments, and live; and my law as the apple of thine eye. Bind them upon thy fingers, write them upon the table of thine heart. Say unto wisdom, Thou art my sister; and call understanding thy kinswoman: That they may keep thee from the strange woman, from the stranger which flattereth with her words. For at the window of my house I looked through my casement, And beheld among the simple ones, I discerned among the youths, a young man void of understanding, Passing through the street near her corner; and he went the way to her house, In the twilight, in the evening, in the black and dark night: And, behold, there met him a woman with the attire of an harlot, and subtil of heart. She is loud and stubborn; her feet abide not in her house: Now is she without, now in the streets, and lieth in wait at every corner. So she caught him, and kissed him, and with an impudent face said unto him, I have peace offerings with me; this day have I payed my vows. Therefore came I forth to meet thee, diligently to seek thy face, and I have found thee. I have decked my bed with coverings of tapestry, with carved works, with fine linen of Egypt. I have perfumed my bed with myrrh, aloes, and cinnamon. Come, let us take our fill of love until the morning: let us solace ourselves with loves. For the goodman is not at home, he is gone a long journey: He hath taken a bag of money with him, and will come home at the day appointed. With her much fair speech she caused him to yield, with the flattering of her lips she forced him. He goeth after her straightway, as an ox goeth to the slaughter, or as a fool to the correction of the stocks; Till a dart strike through his liver; as a bird hasteth to the snare, and knoweth not that it is for his life. Hearken unto me now therefore, O ye children, and attend to the words of my mouth" (Proverbs 7: 1-24).*

Many young men and young women have experienced what is mentioned in this proverb. I thank God that by His grace he spared me from death or the contraction of some incurable sexually transmitted disease. The graveyards are full of young men and young women who were enticed by the thrill of the flesh—oblivious to the fact that they were signing their own death warrant. I am not speaking exclusively about the young because older men and women can and will succumb to the same temptation if the seeds of sexual perversion planted at a young age are not dealt with.

When you see an adult who is dealing with some type of sexual perversion, most likely the seed was sown at an early age. *"Can a man take fire in his bosom and his clothes not be burned?" (Proverbs 6:27).* The fire of lust will consume and devour, but the fire of God will purge and deliver. In the same manner that a man cannot take fire in his lap without being burned, a man cannot expect to indulge in adultery or other forms of illicit sex without suffering the consequences.

I was sitting in a meeting the other day, and the subject of homosexuality came up. It has long been debated whether or not the homosexual was born that way. I am not going to get into that argument or debate because whether or not the person was born that way is irrelevant; the important thing to understand is that we must all be born again, because "all have sinned and come short of the glory of God and the wages of sin is death." We were all born into this world with a sinful nature, which leads us towards a propensity and a proclivity to sin, and that is why we must all be born again.

The homosexual is no different from anyone else in his need to experience the new birth in Christ Jesus. If he was born that way, he needs to be born again; if he was not born that way, he still needs to be born again. Christians are adamant in their argument that homosexuals are not born that way because God does not create homosexuals. The thing we have to remember is that after Adam's fall, man did not look or act in the manner Adam did before his fall. Since the fall of Adam brought sin upon all men, then the desire for men to lay with other men can be one of the consequences of being in a fallen condition. I believe we will be more effective in our witness if we refuse to get bogged down with "born that way" versus "not born that way" in the debate Christians have with homosexuals.

Homosexuals should not be separated into a category by themselves when the issue of sin is discussed. Homosexuality is a sin like adultery, fornication, pornography, and other forms of sexually deviant behavior. To say someone is born a certain way does not give him a pass on sinful behavior because the seed of sin was planted in all of us through Adam. The Bible is explicit in its condemnation of sexual sin, including homosexuality, but we have to understand that Jesus paid the price for all sin and is calling all people to repentance. Neither should the heterosexual think that he is more righteous than a homosexual because he does not struggle with that sin. Jesus said, *"And thou, Capernaum, which art exalted unto heaven, shalt be brought down to hell: for if the mighty works, which have been done in thee, had been done in Sodom, it would have remained until this day. But I say unto you, that it shall be more tolerable for the land of Sodom in the day of judgment, than for thee" (Matthew 11:22-23).*

Capernaum was Jesus' ministry headquarters after John the Baptist was put in prison, and He is telling the people of Capernaum that the Day of Judgment shall be worse for them than the land of Sodom. The body of Christ does not need to spread condemnation but the love of Jesus. We need to let all sinners know that Christ shed His Blood for all sin, and there is no sin that His blood cannot cleanse. Mankind needs the Blood of Jesus; the rich man, the poor man, the beggar man, and the thief, the lawyer, the doctor, and the Indian chief. There is a plethora of scriptures that deal with the sinfulness of man. *"All we like sheep have gone astray; we have turned everyone to his own way and the LORD hath laid on him the iniquity of us all" (Isaiah 53:6).*

From the time we come out of our mother's womb, we are going our own way. Why does the child steal the cookie from the cookie jar when he is told not to do it? He does it because he wants his own way and does not want to be under authority. Rebellious behavior does not appear out of thin air; it is a seed that is already in the heart of every individual from the time they are conceived. As the child grows and interacts with people, places, and things in society, he will gravitate toward destructive behavior if there is no discipline. Humans are driven by an innate desire to have the things that are forbidden, despite the consequences.

The person trapped in the pit of sexual promiscuity knows he runs the risk of contracting an incurable disease, but he is driven to fulfill the urge, and will risk life and limb to do so. Individuals addicted to heroin, crack, and prescription drugs know the path of destruction they are on, but they ignore all the warning signs and will do anything to get the next high.

Michael Jackson was considered the king of pop. He was one of the greatest dancers, singers, and songwriters the world has ever known. He had adoring fans all around the world. He earned millions of dollars, but he was unable to sleep at night without taking strong doses of sleeping medication. All the talent and all the money and fame that he acquired could not give him peace and rest. His journey ended in death, with his doctor facing involuntary manslaughter charges. It appears that every time you turn on the news, there is a report of some celebrity who has overdosed or died in some drug induced state.

The pursuit of carnal hedonistic pleasures and the temporary thrill they bring will often cause us to throw caution to the wind. The arch-enemy of every Christian, the devil, is an expert on the things that please our flesh. He knows our likes and dislikes; he knows the things that stimulate our senses, and he pulls out all stops to entice us to follow a path that will lead to sin and, subsequently, death. I am not saying in every situation we should just say, "The devil made me do it." I am addressing the root of all deviant behavior and the source of that root. My argument is that all of us have something deep inside of us that we were born with and that thing leads us on a journey of death from the day we are born.

The sinful journey of death is a journey only Jesus Christ can change because He alone has the power to change the nature of the sinner. This is what separates Him from any other spiritual figure who has ever walked the earth. There are many spiritual leaders who have passed through this earth, but none of them had the power or the authority to cleanse our sin. For this reason, Christianity stands alone and has no peer or equal in the realm of faith. People in different cultures might serve different gods and have different ideas about life after death, but we all have one thing in common, and that thing is sin. The common denominator that you will find in all people no matter where they dwell on this earth is sin. Despite what some religions teach, it is an inherent flaw in all humans. Whether it is stealing, lying, cheating, killing, or malice, every human being is born with a sin trait. The question is how we deal with sin.

I believe Jesus is the only way out of a life of sin; the only antidote for the sin nature is the blood of Jesus. *"For the life of the flesh is in the blood: and I have given it to you upon the altar to make atonement for your souls: for it is the blood that maketh atonement for the soul" (Leviticus 17:11).* There can be no atonement for the sinful soul without blood, and the only person whose blood was shed for atonement to be possible is the Lord Jesus Christ. This is the reason why the Christian way is the only way to God. People in the world think we are narrow minded and lack tolerance because we believe Jesus is the way, the truth, and the life, and no one can come to the

Father except through Him. Those people need a revelation of the Blood of Jesus Christ, the Lamb of God. There can be no compromise when it comes to the way of salvation. It was Jesus' body that was beaten beyond recognition, then nailed to a cross, so we must be firm and steadfast in professing the truth—that it is only the Blood of Jesus that can cleanse us from our sin.

CHAPTER 4

My Prison

When I say prison I am not speaking exclusively about a place of physical incarceration because many people's minds are trapped in a mental prison. Some are trapped in marital prisons, while others have bodies that are trapped in a physical prison of infirmity. Whatever the prison, know that God is able to deliver. He has the power to break any and all bondages once we call upon Him.

The Mental Prison: The United Negro College Fund had this slogan when I was growing up: *"A mind is a terrible thing to waste."* They knew an educated mind was the key to lifting people out of the pit and prison of poverty. Many believers are trapped in a mental prison of depression, despair, and degradation because of some traumatic experience from which they have not been healed. Applying the Word of God is the key to mental deliverance. The Apostle Peter wrote, *"Forasmuch then as Christ hath suffered for us in the flesh, arm yourselves likewise with the same mind: for he that hath suffered in the flesh hath ceased from sin" (1 Peter 4:1).* The Greek word for arm is *hoplizo,* and it comes from a root that means *to equip with weapons used for offensive war*. The mind is the battleground for spiritual warfare because the enemy knows if he can ware us down mentally, he will have an easier time defeating us. He knows the joy of the Lord is our strength, and he seeks to sap that strength by replacing our joy with depression.

The Marital Prison: Some couples are trapped in a marital prison because there is no love left. The husband is on one side of the bed and the wife is on the other. They are still living under the same roof, but that is as far as the marriage goes. The marriage lacks luster, and they have been reduced to being roommates instead of soulmates.

I sat with a friend one day, and she told me that her sister had just met a guy. She took him to meet her mother, then gave away her furniture and is ready to marry him. She informed me that her sister hardly knew the guy, but she is ready to move in and marry him. When a couple is dating, there is a great deal of care and concern because each person is trying to win the love and affection of the other—or trying to get to the place of physical intimacy—but there is a big difference between dating someone and living with them in holy matrimony. Couples need to realize that the honeymoon will not last forever, so they'd better count the cost before they say "I do."

The Physical Prison: As foresaid, I am not referring only to a physical place of incarceration here but also to a person whose strong mind may be imprisoned in a body that is ailing from a debilitating disease. Once again, it is the application of the Word of God in the life of the individual that will allow him to rise above the physical limitations. You might be limited in your mobility, but you must constantly remind yourself of the scripture that says, *"For this corruptible must put on incorruption and this mortal must put on immortality" (1Corinthians 15:53).* Whatever the pit, whatever the prison, know that God can and will deliver you in due season.

I learned of God's deliverance first hand because I suffered from my own prison experiences. Before I went into the prison of my incarceration, I had to deal with a mental, marital, and an emotional prison.

God strategically positioned Joseph in the prison so he could interpret the chief butler's dream, which would eventually lead him to the palace. Prison was the place God allowed me to go so He could save me for the work that he had for me. Unlike Joseph, it was my propensity to succumb to my fleshly inclinations, which led me to prison, but God can shine his light in the darkest of places.

The Story Behind the Glory

Like everyone else, I have my battles with my old carnal nature, which tries, constantly, to rise. Although I am a new creature in Christ, my sanctification is ongoing, and the Holy Ghost helps me win the battle when the old nature rises. The only time I lose is when I try to fight the battle by myself. We can't defeat the devil in the realm of the flesh because that is where he is strongest.

I often think of the times in my life before I was in a covenant relationship with the Lord. At that time, I was totally under the control of my carnal nature, and readily gave in to its whims and desires. As a matter of fact, I have to shake my head in disbelief when I think of some of the places my sinful desires took me and some of the things I found myself doing. If someone came to me when I was a child and told me that I would be sentenced to eight years in an English prison for drug smuggling, I would have told them they were out of their mind.

I did not start on the journey that led me to places like Wormwood Scrubs and Brixton prison right away. Little sins led to bigger sins until I found myself in places and situations for which I was not prepared. The carnal appetite is insatiable, and once you start feeding it, it will not be satisfied. It's like the person who starts out smoking cigarettes to look cool, then graduates to smoking marijuana, then graduates to using heroin, sniffing coke, or smoking crack cocaine. I am sure it was not the intention of that person to become an addict, driven to unspeakable things to get the next fix—stealing from family members or anyone else who left their possessions unguarded, selling their bodies to get the next hit. The person escalates their drug use to get a better high, but once they are hooked, they have to use the drug to try to get back to the place of normalcy.

I remember seeing the heroin addicts in the seventies. There was a methadone clinic in the neighborhood where they went for treatment. When they were under the influence of the drug, they looked as if they were about to fall asleep; they did something called "the dope fiend lean." They would lean over as if they were about to hit the floor, but amazingly enough, they were able to stay on their feet.

The eighties brought a proliferation of crack cocaine, which brought a great deal of carnage to many inner-city neighborhoods. I've heard that this form of cocaine is so potent you could get hooked by one hit of the pipe. It turned men and women into zombies who would be out at night scouring the streets, looking for their next hit.

I had no idea of the turn my own life would take once I started hanging out with unsavory characters. I guess I should have known because my mom always said, "Show me your company, and I will tell you who you are. Birds of a feather flock together. What drops off the head drops on the shoulders. The apple doesn't fall far from the tree."

My life was promising before I went off on a tangent and ended up in left field. I was born on the island of Jamaica in July of 1962. My mom moved to the United States and settled in Corona Queens, where my brothers and sisters and I came to live with her. I had a tough time in the neighborhood and in school because I spoke English with a Jamaican accent. I was teased in school because I didn't have the latest fashion, and when I went out of the neighborhood to high school, I had to deal with the white kids that called us niggers. I couldn't catch a break because in my own neighborhood, I was ostracized and told that I'd come to America on a boat, and outside of the neighborhood I was attacked because of the color of my skin.

I tried my best to adapt to the American culture, but after visiting Jamaica for the first time since I'd left as a young boy, I was smitten by the culture. I started listening to reggae music and hung out with other West Indians. The type of reggae I loved was what is called dance hall music. In the dance hall, the operator plays the record while the DJ chants his lyrics. The dance hall lyrics were graphic in their description of how to display your sexual prowess by bedding as many women as possible, smoking the best ganja (marijuana), and firing the biggest gun. The dance hall culture is very hedonistic and is all about satisfying the flesh. There were DJs that made cultural songs, but my favorite was the rude boy style.

Only what's inside a man can come out of him, so I should not have been surprised when I started to live out the scenes that were described in my favorite records. It was all about pleasing the flesh, and I wanted as much fleshly pleasure as I could get. I frequented local parties in the neighborhood, drank rum, and slept around. After awhile, I started hanging on the corner with the tough guys in the neighborhood, and before I knew it, I was doing the same things they were doing. Association brings on assimilation, and I guess that's what my grandmother meant when she said, "If you lay down with dogs, you will get up with flees." Grandma probably didn't know it, but there are much more dangerous things you can get up with now, things that are incurable, such as Herpes, Syphilis, and AIDS. There was a lot of promiscuity in the eighties because women would sell their bodies to get crack. I don't believe most people realized at that time that AIDS could be contracted through heterosexual acts. Most of us thought it was a disease that was spread through Homosexual activities and intravenous drug use.

The DJ KRS One had a song titled, "Super Hoe." In one of his other songs, he said, *"The girlies are free but the crack cost money."* I had the free girlies because I had the crack, and it is only because of the mercy and grace of God that I did not contract AIDS. How ironic; the God that I refused to serve is the one that kept me from losing my life during those turbulent years. He is truly rich in mercy.

Stay in an environment long enough and you will develop a tolerance for that environment. The more I hung on the corner with the crew, the more I wanted to hang on the corner with the crew. They had the nice cars, the expensive clothes, and were surrounded by all the women. Nobody messed with us because there were guys in our midst that were cold blooded; they would shoot or stab you for the slightest infraction or show of disrespect. I have been in houses where multiple people were shot, both male and female. Something in me knew that the lifestyle in which I was entangled was a very destructive one, but my desire to be in the midst of the players deadened my senses to the destruction that lay beneath the surface.

One of my childhood friends used to say, "Live fast, die young, and make a beautiful corpse." Young people need to understand that all that glitters is not gold. On the surface, the life of the pimp or the dope pusher might look glamorous, but ninety-nine percent of them wind up dead, in prison, or as police informants. I didn't know it at the time, but I would be exposed to all three. I would wind up in prison, lose friends to the grim reaper, and be the victim of informants. A person can be the most feared, revered gangster, but when the police get a hold of most of them and tell them they are going to do twenty-five years to life, or life in prison without the possibility of parole, they start squealing faster and louder than a stuck pig. The drug dealer or other criminals might have a sense of benevolence because they give money to kids in the neighborhood, hand out turkeys on

Thanksgiving, or presents at Christmas, but the effect crime has on the community negates any good that a criminal can do.

In Jamaica, where I was born, there are garrison communities that are run by a "don." He is usually someone under the control of one of the political parties. He uses any means necessary to control the community. Many of these so-called dons are responsible for murders and other ghastly acts. Many of these people are looked upon by the masses not as criminals but as heroes. Their exploits are glorified in music, and many young men strive to be like them. These individuals are not heroes; they are zeroes. At this very moment, there is a community in Jamaica named Tivoli Gardens that is under siege because the United States is trying to extradite the don of the community. The irony is, the individual's father faced extradition and supposedly died in a mysterious fire in a Jamaican jail in April of 1992. The community of Tivoli Gardens and other areas of western Kingston are under siege at the present time because the gunmen in the community have decided the police and soldiers will have to kill them before they allow them to arrest him. Police stations have been burned, and several police officers and others have been killed. Innocent citizens will continue to lose their lives because of one man.

One man, whether he is good or bad, can have a positive or a negative effect on a community. A person can be a murderer, but if he provides services in the community that the government cannot or will not provide, he will be looked upon as a hero, not a zero.

"Poverty makes strange bed fellows." When people are poor, and they dwell in a pit of poverty and destitution, they do not really care if the person feeding them is a drug smuggler, murderer, or otherwise. They will sear their consciousness because their primary concern is where their next meal is coming from, not the moral turpitude of the individual who feeds them.

You know a society is in trouble when there are certain areas into which the police are not willing to go because the don, his cohorts, and henchmen are heavily armed. A politician or a law enforcement personnel that is in league with a criminal is worse than that criminal because the criminal is doing what criminals do, but the other two are sworn to protect and to serve. The problem with crime in Jamaica and other countries is politicians who take money from the strongmen in the garrison communities, and underpaid police officers who are corrupt.

My mother tried her best to warn me, but I would have none of it. She constantly stressed education, and before my life got totally out of control, I graduated from high school and enrolled in one of the City Universities. In my freshman year, I spent a lot of my time in the student union because that is where the party was. When I realized that in college, your hands are not held like they are in high school, I started putting some effort into my schoolwork. But I left school one class shy of graduation and moved to the Bronx because my girlfriend was pregnant. When my daughter Tierra was born, I was ecstatic but unprepared for fatherhood. I did not have the maturity level to do what I needed to do for her. To this day, I lament the fact that I was not there for my first child as I should have been. My dad taught me that a person cannot take back a spent coin or a spoken word, so I try not to dwell on it. Her mother did a wonderful job with her, and despite being born and raised in the south Bronx, she was able to graduate cum laude from Binghamton University—go Tierra. I love you, and I am very proud of what you have accomplished.

Like fatherhood, I was totally unprepared for marriage and thought "I do" meant I could do whatever I did before I got married. I had no concept of the importance of honoring the marriage vows. A person can be sincere in their desire to honor their marriage vows, but soul ties and deviant behavior do not cease because a person said "I do." We have to be delivered from certain thought patterns and habits that facilitate negative behavior. Whatever area in which you are weak before the marriage will manifest in the marriage if steps are not taken to deal with those areas. My area of weakness was lust because for many years, the lifestyle of a drug dealer meant a steady stream of women. I was married but was not delivered from the streets, or from fornication. When you are married and have not been delivered from lust and perversion, fornication turns to adultery. I was married to my wife, but I was also married to the streets.

Like The Crusaders sang, "Street life, it's the only life I know," Actually, it's the only life I wanted to know because it was exciting and intoxicating. Isn't that the way sin is? It seduces you, intoxicates you, and then it destroys you. The devil knows the areas in which to tempt us, because he knows the flavor that whets our fleshly appetite, and without the power of the Holy Ghost, it is impossible to resist all his temptations. *"Blessed is the man that endureth temptation: for when he is tried, he shall receive the crown of life, which the Lord hath promised to them that love him. Let no man say when he is tempted, I am tempted of God: for God cannot be tempted with evil, neither tempteth he any man: But every man is tempted, when he is drawn away of his own lust, and enticed. Then when lust hath conceived, it bringeth forth sin: and sin, when it is finished, bringeth forth death"* (James 1: 12-15).

Adam and Eve walked and talked with God in a beautiful garden in the cool of the day, and the serpent was able to beguile Eve and cause Adam to rebel by twisting the word God gave them. An individual without the Word of God is powerless to resist the devil. It does not matter how intelligent he is. David declared, *"Thy word have I hid in mine heart, that I might not sin against thee"* (Psalm 119:11). David sent Uriah to the front of the battle field so he would be killed in order to cover up that fact that he had impregnated his wife. The devil is not to be played with. Sin may seem pleasurable for a season, but I was about to find out that the season of pleasure is short, while the bitterness can last a lifetime.

The Apostle James declared, *"When lust has conceived it bringeth forth sin."* We were born of a corruptible seed because of Adam's transgression, and our adversary, the devil, knows exactly what to entice us with. In my heart, I was lusting for the fast lifestyle. Through that lust, sin was conceived and began to manifest when I bought drugs and started dealing, just like the players on the corner. They were the movers and shakers, and I wanted a piece of the action. Before I knew it, I had built a lifestyle around drug dealing and whore-mongering, and I must be honest—it was sweet to the soul, but I was about to find out that what is sweet to the soul will eventually be bitter to the stomach.

I graduated from selling nickel and dime bags on the corner to selling marijuana by the pound. The devil will provide opportunities for growth to draw you deeper and deeper into your sin. I had a friend that worked as a baggage handler in the airport, and at that time people were carrying suitcases loaded with marijuana from

Texas to New York. My friend and some of his co-workers would steal the suitcases, and I would buy it from them and resell it. I was the man because I had the quantity. I was able to buy expensive jewelry; I wore fine clothing and cavorted with many women. Things looked glamorous on the surface but were rotten beneath it. When the pipeline for marijuana dried up, I graduated to selling crack cocaine because I had developed a certain lifestyle I did not want to give up. Although the penalty for dealing crack was more stringent than for marijuana, I took the risk because the payoff was greater.

Because the lifestyle of a crack dealer was much more dangerous than when I dealt marijuana, I had to arm myself with guns—after all, everyone else was armed. When you are in the midst of a fast and dangerous lifestyle, it is very difficult to spot the warning signs because you are totally consumed by the pleasures that lifestyle brings. There were plenty of warnings, like the time I was traveling from Texas with a car trunk full of guns and drugs and the muffler was blowing a great deal of smoke because of engine problems. If the police had pulled us over, we would have gone to prison for a long time. We made it to New York with the drugs, but the person who was supposed to buy the drugs set up the person to whom we meant to sell it, and the drugs were stolen. My friends and I decided to go to the house of the person who had stolen the drugs.

We went to the house one night and hid in the backyard waiting for an opportunity to storm the house. We were heavily armed and wanted revenge. It is only by the grace of God that the occupants of the house were kept alive. We found out that the guy was not home and only a female and some children were in the house, so we left.

Then there was the time I went on trial in New York, and they locked me up right before the verdict was announced. Everyone thought the case was lost, but the jury came back with a not guilty verdict. Instead of counting my blessings and changing my life, I was back on the corner drinking and celebrating the temporary victory with my cronies. With every escape, I became a more brazen criminal. There is a sense of invincibility when a person is living on the edge because without it, I would not have been able to take some of the daring chances that I took.

It did not matter that people's lives were being destroyed by the potent poison I was selling; it didn't matter that people were being killed or sent to prison for a long time. I couldn't see beyond my own narcissistic lifestyle. When I found out that I could make more money smuggling drugs to England, I became a transcontinental drug smuggler. I got my practice smuggling drugs from Jamaica to New York and Canada, and now it was time to cross the Atlantic Ocean. I got away with it the first time and was emboldened by the proceeds I received. Most people were moving drugs from state to state in the United States, which was very risky. If the Feds did not get you, then someone would probably set you up to be robbed and killed. Going overseas was less risky, and the pound was worth much more than the dollar—so from a business perspective, it seemed like a good move.

Warning comes before destruction and a haughty spirit before a fall. I remember the night I was searching for my passport because I was going to make my last trip to England. It was in the month of November, and because Christmas was around the corner, I needed some money fast. Christmas was supposed to be about the birth of Christ, but for me it was all about the presents—not His presence. I was furious when I could not find my passport. I accused my wife of hiding it and used some choice words to let her know how furious I was. I can hear her words now as if it were yesterday. She said, "Fidel, the Lord does not want you to go, and that is why you cannot find it." Her words fell on deaf ears because I had no interest in the Lord she served. I know there are many that would be alive or free today if only they had listened to the wife, mother, father, or friend who was telling them not to do what they were about to do. When my children were younger, I told them to be careful of the company they kept. I told them, many kids are dead or in prison for a long time because they got in the car and thought they were going for a ride. They did not leave home with a plan to rob someone or sell drugs, but the fact that they were in the car made them an accessory to the crime. My life would have been a lot different if I had listened to my wife, but I thank God that things turned out the way they did.

I searched for hours and when I found it, I told my wife, "Yes, I found it; God wants me to go." I was being sarcastic of course, but

God would get the last laugh. He who laughs last laughs best, and a sinner will not get the last laugh.

England, Here I Come

My childhood friend and I boarded a flight the next day and headed to England. In the cab on the way to the airport, we drank, laughed, and planned what we would do with the proceeds from our crime. *"For when they shall say, peace and safety; then sudden destruction cometh upon them, as travail upon a woman with child; and they shall not escape." (1 Thes 5:3).* I wish I had known that verse before I took the trip; then again, it probably would not have mattered because I was on a collision course with destiny—nothing could stop it.

We were able to get by immigration and customs with the drugs, but the person who was supposed to pick us up at the airport did not show. I found out later that he felt the police were watching him. I had to revert to plan B because hanging around the airport with a half kilo of cocaine is not the wisest thing to do. A friend of mine had a girlfriend living in South London and made arrangements for us to stop off at her house. I was totally oblivious to the fact that she lived in a notorious part of South London, which was infested by drugs. Scotland Yard (English Police) was watching her house. I was stepping into a trap that would change my life forever. When a person is planning a crime or in the midst of committing the crime, they are focused on getting away with the spoils, but I don't believe most of us count the cost. If the person serving a life sentence or the person on death row knew that the outcome would be what it turned out to be, they would probably have done something different. Unfortunately, there is no crystal ball to look into that will tell a person when they will get caught. The best thing to do is not to commit any crimes. If a person does decide to commit the crime, they better be willing to pay the price if they are caught.

Crime Does Not Pay, It Costs

I went to the Florida Department of Corrections website to find the cost of housing each inmate in the state of Florida, and here is what I found. *"It costs $55.09 on average per day or $20,108 per year to keep an inmate in prison. Most of the daily cost to incarcerate an* inmate in a major prison is spent on security and medical services. The remaining 20% or so is spent on feeding, clothing and education for the inmates, and some administrative issues. A total of 8.5% of the state general revenue budget goes to corrections in Florida, which has a budget of more than two billion dollars. $1.47 billion of that goes directly toward security and institutional operations, and another $424 million toward health services for inmates, including mental health and dental care."

Criminal activities cost society on a whole, and the cost cannot be estimated solely in financial terms. Most people who commit crimes don't stop to consider the toll their crime takes on society, their families, and even themselves once they are caught.

The realness of the statement, "Crime does not pay, it costs," hit home when I was arrested for smuggling drugs into England. It cost society billions of dollars a year to keep criminals incarcerated. It costs the families of the inmates time, resources, and emotions as they try to go on with life with a loved one who is behind bars. In that respect, the family members are doing time along with the inmate because so much of their time, energy, and resources are spent visiting their loved ones, putting money in their accounts, and praying for their safe return. I witnessed the heartache and the thousands of dollars my mom spent to try to help my oldest brother when he kept getting in trouble. You would think that I would have kept my nose clean and spared my loved ones the anguish felt when a family member is imprisoned.

I have a friend who was convicted of a serious crime, and his mother exhausted her life savings to work on his appeal. Fortunately for both of them, it appears that he was wrongfully convicted and a judge has ruled that he can get a new trial. He has already been incarcerated for over a decade. He lost his business, his wife, and of course he cannot get the time back that he has spent behind bars. Only God knows the emotional toll that incarnation takes upon the inmate and his family. Please do not get me wrong; I believe if you do the crime then you should be willing to do the time. It is the innocent children who are left without a parent or parents who concern me. Many children are more likely to engage in criminal activity because they don't have a father figure in the house; many of them are in poverty because their father's life of crime has caused him to be missing from their lives. There are many inmates who were not around for the formative growth years of their children. The toll on children who have to grow up without their fathers is a great one. Children are not the only ones who suffer from the incarceration of a loved one.

What about the mother, girlfriend, or wife who spends untold hours traveling just to make the next visit? What about the fact that they spend their hard earned money to pay lawyers? Lawyers who, at times, are in cahoots with overzealous prosecutors and judges who want to further their careers by showing they are tough on crime by handing out lengthy sentences. I don't think the person who is doing the time realizes the costs and the burden their families have to bear. When you look at the cumulative effect that a person's crime has on society and their family, it makes you wonder why anyone would commit another crime after being released from prison.

Some inmates pay the ultimate price when they are murdered or raped by other inmates. Prison is more about keeping dangerous criminals off the streets than it is about rehabilitation. Rehabilitation can only begin when the inmate decides in his mind that he has had enough of his life of crime. Then, he decides to work hard at reconstructing his life. Reconstruction is difficult because of the stigma that is attached to anyone convicted of a crime. In many instances, it is very difficult for the person to find a job because they have a criminal record. Sometimes they go right back to their former lifestyle, and that is why the recidivism rate is so high. Some inmates get so acclimated to life in prison that they find it difficult to reintegrate back into society. They get accustomed to the controlled prison environment—especially if they had any authority there. I don't know why anyone would prefer to be locked up with a bunch of men, but I knew many people growing up who did long stretches in prison, came out, and went back within a couple of months or less.

For the majority of people who commit crimes, money spent to incarcerate them is well spent because criminals with minds that are not transformed will go back to committing more crimes as soon as they are released. Let's be honest, who wants a pedophile, a rapist, or a serial killer loose in their neighborhood? I am sure people say the same about a drug dealer, a car thief, and a bank robber. I believe in rehabilitation, I just do not believe that prisons do a good job in that area, and the recidivism rate backs up my assertion. When an individual goes to prison, he encounters other people of larcenous proclivity, and stories of criminal exploits are exchanged. In many instances, connections are made between the inmates, which they plan on utilizing when they get out.

A true spiritual epiphany is one of the ways in which an inmate is changed. Other inmates come to the realization that crime does not pay and they need to change their lives, but those inmates are few and far between. The person who decides to go straight will have a hard time because society frowns upon people who have criminal records. You pay the proverbial debt to society, but you are discriminated against in the job market because of a lack of trust. It is like the person is doing double time. They do their time, but when they get out they also suffer. Those who want to work find it difficult to get gainful employment. Many of them become frustrated, take matters into their own hands, and wind up right back where they started.

I bought and sold clothes when I first got out of prison before I found a job. I was blessed by the fact that my arrest and conviction were in England, and the record did not follow me to the United States. There are people who are in prison who, if given the chance, will keep their nose clean and work to become productive members of society, but they have to be given a chance. If you get out of prison and you can not find a decent job, start your own business. Do everything possible to keep from going back to a penile institution.

Unfortunately, many inmates are waiting for their opportunity to get out so they can get back to their hustle. In their minds, they feel that the next time around they will be more careful, and they will not be caught. Some inmates actually have enough connections in the streets to continue to run their criminal enterprise from behind bars. The person committing crimes needs to know that the people with whom they are committing crimes will sell them out in a heartbeat. When faced with the prospect of spending years in jail, some people will sell out their mother, wife, sister, or brother. I am not saying that all inmates are like that, but a chain is only as strong as its weakest link, and there is always a weak link in the crew. Many people are languishing in prison today because someone they thought they could trust had a wire on, which allowed police to listen to their conversation. Once the police or the feds get a hold of the weak link, they will sing like a canary. Sammy the Bull Gravano murdered many people, but when he was caught, he had no qualms about informing on his boss, John Gotti.

Prisons are not full of choir boys, although some boys in prison sing in the choir. Prison is a place where you are surrounded by other criminals who will stab you in the back or bludgeon you with an instrument if you let down your guard. I was about to witness that first-hand in one of the places in which I would be housed while in England. Prison is not a place for the weak or the faint of heart. I found that out after the house in which I was staying was raided early in the morning, after we had just gotten in from what the English call a rave. A rave is a party that goes on into the early hours of the morning. I was intoxicated and ill-prepared for the battering ram Scotland Yard was using to beat down the door of the apartment. Either Scotland Yard knew we were in there with drugs, or they were making a bust because of a deal that had gone down before we got there. Whatever the case may have been, my whole world was about to be turned upside down. My heart raced, my mind reeled as I ran downstairs and began to flush the cocaine down the toilet. The toilet was right next to the door they were pounding, and the pounding sounded like it was inside my head. It was so much cocaine that they gained entry to the apartment before I could flush it all down the toilet. The prophetic words of my mother, my wife, my friends, and everyone that had ever warned me was now coming to pass. I was busted and would have to pay the piper.

I was sitting in the police station being interrogated by Scotland Yard and feeling like I was trapped in some terrible nightmare. After the interrogation, I was transferred to one of the prisons to sit on remand until my court date.

Don't Do the Crime If You Can't Do the Time
There I was in Wormwood Scrubs, a notorious British prison that looked more like a dungeon than anything else. Gone were the gold chains, the diamond rings, the Moet Champagne, the fancy night

clubs, and the women who frequented those clubs. I was on twenty-three-hour-a-day lock down in a cell that had no toilet. I could hear the words of my wife ringing in my ears when she used to say, "Stop doing what you are doing; give your heart to Jesus and go to church with me." My response to her was, "Get out of here with that white man's religion, because fools go to church on Sunday." I would have gladly gone to church on Sunday with her if I could just get out of that wretched place. I realized very early on that people who were arrested for sexual crimes like rape did not fare too well in English prisons. Those particular inmates were called "nunces," and they were beaten on a regular basis. I remember standing near a pool table in one of the places I was remanded. All of a sudden there was a commotion, and when I looked around I saw a man with blood running down the side of his face by his ear. He appeared as if he was in shock, and he kept saying, "I was just standing there, and they attacked me." Of course no one saw the attack because in prison, an informant does not fare too well either. The inmates charged with sexual crimes did not want anyone to know what they are in for, but prison guards tell other inmates their dirty little secret. After being attacked, the inmate would either be transferred to another prison or sent to protective custody.

My lifestyle had thrust me into a world that I wanted to be out of as quickly as possible. I could think of a lot better ways to spend my time than to be locked up with a bunch of men. My thought was, "There is no fun in the bull pen unless there are some heifers in there." Deep down on the inside, I knew that I was not going anywhere for awhile. I kept remembering the slogan, **"DON'T DO THE CRIME IF YOU CAN'T DO THE TIME."**

Absentee Husband and Father

The worst part about being arrested was not the loss of freedom and the prospect of being locked away for many years, although I must admit, the whole idea was very unsettling. In the back of my mind, I knew my luck would run out one day. My hope was that when it did, I would not end up on some street corner, my body riddled with bullets. I also hoped that I would not be sentenced to so much time that I would be old and grey by the time I was released—*if* I was released. The most difficult part of my incarceration was coming to the realization that I had failed miserably as a husband and a father. I had left my first daughter, Tierra, because of selfishness and immaturity, and now I was away from my wife and the children we had together because of my criminal activities. It took me almost a year before I could call home. Prior to that, all communication was through writing. I just could not bear the thought of hearing the voices of my children and falling apart. Truthfully speaking, I was not a candidate for father of the year even when I was free because I spent many hours away from my wife and children—hustling and partying was more important to me at the time.

My mind was in such a sinful state that I could not see the neglect I was causing my family. You can't put a premium on the importance of just spending quality time with your children. My wife is a great mother, but how could she teach boys how to be men? They needed me to help them through the difficulties of life, but I was busy doing my own thing. Now I was locked up in a foreign country, which made it impossible to be there even if I wanted to.

I became another negative statistic, another black man who had abandoned his family, leaving them to depend on the welfare system to get by. I didn't have much money stashed away because I spent it as fast as it came in. There were times when I was driven to despair at the thought of my children suffering as a result of my stupidity. I remember the time I called home for the first time, and the affect it had on me. It was wonderful to hear the voice of my precious wife. When my son Mario got on the phone, he asked me a question that pierced my heart and filled my eyes with tears. Mario said, "Daddy, when are you coming home?" I was at a loss for words because his question caught me off guard. To this day when I think of that moment, my eyes fill up with tears. When I got back to my cell, I wept like a baby, but I made a decision that day. The decision was, if or when the prison doors opened, I would work hard to repair any and all damage caused by my incarceration.

I am happy to report that today, May 1, 2010, I had the privilege of watching Mario graduate from the University of West Florida with a degree in business. Last year, Tierra received her masters' degree in education, and my daughter Makeda received her Bachelor's degree in psychology. My other two children, Malik and Shante, are High School graduates, and I hope they go on to college. Hallelujah!!!

While in England, things got worse before they got better. While on remand, I found out that I was named in a conspiracy case in the Midwest that could send me to prison for life. It is one thing when you get that kind of news when you are free, but I got the news when I was already in prison, so I could not run or hide. My life was crumbling quickly, and if I did not receive a miracle, prison was going to be my home for a very long time.

I did not give much thought to the idea of life in prison when I was free because I was too wrapped up in the street life. With the loss of my freedom, I was forced to deal with the reality of my present dilemma and the choices that led me there.

CHAPTER 5

Somebody Prayed for Me

It appeared as if my goose was cooked, but unbeknownst to me, there were many people praying and interceding for me. When intercessors get you in their crosshairs and begin to bombard heaven for you, God will hear their cries and deliver you.

My sister Janet met with a friend named Colleen on Thursdays, and they prayed for me. Janet was the first person among my brothers and sisters to be saved. We used to mock and criticize her, but she stood firm in her faith. No one knew that she would be one of the many intercessors the Lord would use to pray us into His Kingdom. She is a testament of the fact that persistent prayer pays off. She is the Joseph in our family in the sense that she was attacked by her brothers and sisters for her faith. When you are the only one amongst your siblings standing for Jesus, the devil will use the others against you. Although she was mocked and ridiculed, she remained steadfast because of the discipline she'd learned at the church she attended. She was saved in and attended a church called Tabernacle, which is located on Jamaica Avenue in Queens, New York. The pastor was a no nonsense man of God named Apostle Johnny Washington. He was serious about the things of God, and God honored his steadfastness by placing a great apostolic prophetic anointing on his life.

At Tabernacle, they had one hour of prayer before every service, fifty days of consecration every year, and a one-day fast every week. It was the kind of environment Janet needed because after she left church, she had to come home and deal with the devils that used her siblings to attack her.

The Psalmist said, *"God setteth the solitary in families; He bringeth out those that are bound with chains, but the rebellious dwell in a dry land" (Psalm 68:6).* Dr. Mark Hanby ministered at our church on Psalm 68, and I received great insight on this verse. The solitary is a precious diamond. He said it is like a jeweler setting the diamond in place. He said diamonds can cut steal. I was fascinated by the statement because Psalm 68 declares, *"He bringeth out those that are bound with chains."* Janet was a diamond in the rough, whom the Lord saved, polished, and used to cut the steel chains that held us bound. My siblings and I did not understand that our rebellion caused us to be in a dry place. Out of ignorance, we persecuted the one the Lord had set in our family as a solitary. God set Janet in our family to intercede for us so the chains would be broken. Janet did not beat us over the head with scriptures; she prayed until the chains began to break.

Janet received her mantle from our Paternal Pentecostal grandmother who rose at five o'clock every morning to pray. The people in the neighborhood called her Mother Mack. She was like an alarm clock because the people in the area could hear her praying and singing the song of the Lord early in the morning. She was so zealous and steadfast for the things of God that she turned part of her house into a church. My grandmother told Janet that God promised to save all her grandchildren. A promise is a comfort to a fool, but when the promise is from God, you can take it to the bank—His promises are yeah and amen. My grandmother once told me the Lord promised her length of days in the earth, and He fulfilled that promise because she lived to be one hundred and two.

Everyone should pray, but I believe intercessors are birthed into the ministry of intercessory prayer. They have an uncanny ability to stand in the gap and labor in prayer until there is a breakthrough. Intercessors have the discipline to turn down their plates for long periods of time. Fasting is necessary because some cases are so difficult that the breakthrough requires fasting and prayer. An intercessor is one who prays to God on behalf of others.

When Jesus came down from the mount of transfiguration, He was approached by a man asking Him to have mercy on his son. The man described his son as a lunatic who fell into fire and water on many occasions because he was sore vexed. The father told Jesus that he brought his son to the disciples, but they could not cure him. The Lord told them to "bring him hither to me." Jesus rebuked the devil and cast it out of the child and the Bible says, "the child was cured from that very hour." The disciples came to Jesus and asked him why they could not cast out the devil? And Jesus said unto them, *"...because of your unbelief: for verily I say unto you, if ye have faith as a grain of mustard seed, ye shall say unto this mountain, remove hence to yonder place; and it shall remove; and nothing shall be impossible unto you. Howbeit this kind goeth not out but by prayer and fasting"* (Luke 17: 20-21).

If you are going to worry then don't bother praying, and if you are going to pray, then don't worry. When we approach God in prayer, we must believe that He will answer. We can't approach God with our prayers in unbelief and expect to get positive results. Jesus let the disciples know that unbelief was a problem, but dealing with that type of devil also required fasting. Years later, I would be on a mission trip in Porus, in Jamaica. There was a lady there that was experiencing severe stomach problems, which she attributed to someone working witchcraft on her. One of the team members requested that we pray for her. We were in a room, and he kept on saying the blood of Jesus, the blood of Jesus. After awhile, he said if any of us in the room were afraid we could wait outside. I went outside, not because I was afraid but because the room was hot, and we were all sweating; it was obvious to me and a few others that the methodology was not working. Jesus did not have to labor and sweat to cast out a devil. The blood of Jesus is given for the remission of sins, but the power to cast out devils is in the name of Jesus because demons are subject to us in His name. A day or two later, I was ministering at the night service and the anointing was there to destroy yokes. While ministering, I saw the young lady and summoned her to come forth. I looked at her and said, "In the name of Jesus I command you to come out." As soon as I said it, she upchucked, which means she vomited up this unrecognizable mass, and was set free instantly.

My sister believed that God would set me free from sin and deliver me from the prison cell. She fasted and prayed without ceasing for me, and I have no doubt that it was that dedication to fasting and prayer by her and my wife Paulette that opened the door for salvation for me and the eventual deliverance from the English prison. I am a product of prayer; I was set free because somebody prayed for me. I believe tenacious, persistent intercessory prayer is one of the key things missing from many churches today. Believers must learn to pray without ceasing.

In the parable of the unjust judge, Jesus said, *"Men ought always to pray, and not to faint" (Luke 18:1b)*. He said men ought to pray, but it seems the majority of the prayer warriors I come across in churches are women, and I thank God for them. In the parable, Jesus talked about a judge in a city, which did not fear God or have any regard for man. There was a widow that kept appearing in the court of the judge, pestering him to avenge her of her adversary. At first the judge would not comply, but after a while he said, *"Though I fear not God, nor regard man; yet because this widow troubleth me, I will avenge her, lest by her continual coming she weary me" (Luke 18: 4-5)*. When the judge says lest she weary me, in the Greek it literally means, *lest she give me a black eye*. Jesus gave that parable to teach us how we should be persistent in our prayers, and our persistence will get us answers to our prayers. Jesus went on to say, *"And shall not God avenge His own elect, which cry day and night unto Him, though He bear long with them?"* (Luke 18:7). God has elected some to be intercessors and given them grace to cry out to him day and night. These warriors in prayer will not faint because the answer to prayer is a long time coming. They have been called by the Lord to stand in the gap for others. Intercessors are like that widow in Luke 18; their prayers are like a battering ram beating down doors in the heavenly realm.

While my sister Janet and her prayer partners were praying, my wife Paulette, her sister, her aunt, and the intercessors from her church were also interceding for me. God will extend His grace to a sinner and protect that sinner from being killed because sanctified, consecrated saints are praying. I know there were many times when I should have been killed, but God had mercy on me because a righteous wife, sister, and their prayer team bombarded Heaven for me. I remember the nights I would come home drunk and find my wife and her prayer partners in the living room having prayer. I was in a wretched condition, but I knew that I should not interrupt them. I remember coming home and staggering to my room. Years later, my wife told me that she would anoint me with oil while I was sleeping and pray over me. I am sure there are many husbands and also children who were oiled down by some intercessor who kept them on the altar.

Husbands with saved wives need to treat them royally because a husband's prayers can be hindered due to the way in which he treats his wife. Husbands should treat their wives well whether or not their wives are saved, but it is important to reiterate the fact that if the wife is saved, then there is a correlation between answered prayers and how he treats her. Let me give you the scripture reference. *"Likewise, ye husbands deal with them according to knowledge, giving honour unto the wife, as unto the weaker vessel, and as being heirs together of the grace of life; that your prayers be not hindered" (1 Peter 3:7).* I wish I'd known and followed that scripture because it would have spared my wife a great deal of heartache and pain. Of course, being saved would have helped because a saved man who loves Jesus will follow Jesus' command to every husband to love his wife like He loved the church and gave His life for it. There is a two-fold command given to husbands and wives by the Lord. Husbands are to love their wives like Christ loved the Church and gave Himself for it, and wives are to submit themselves unto their own husbands as unto the Lord.

Because of abuse and excess, the word "submit" has become a dirty word. A wife should not submit herself to a husband who is abusive because the scripture clearly says, "as unto the Lord." This means the person being submitted to should be walking in the love of Jesus. Submit is not for the purpose of the husband dominating and bossing the wife around; it is in the context of a covering and a loving protective head. I heard a friend of mine say, "No woman wants to submit to King Kong." A husband should not expect to be treated like prince charming when he is acting like a Gorilla. Godly submission does not mean you stay in a situation where you are suffering verbal, emotional, or physical abuse. I have heard stories where women are told in counseling sessions that they should stay in the marriage despite the physical abuse because the Lord will deliver the husband. Excuse me! When someone is busting you upside the head, you'd better run for your life as fast as you can. I am not advocating for a wife to leave her husband on a whim because there are problems in the marriage, but obviously a woman should extricate herself from any situation where her life is in danger. I have personally witnessed situations where women stayed in marriages through years of terrible physical beatings only to be abandoned by the husband when he needed a new punching bag. Some would say those women suffered from battered women's syndrome.

Husbands need to go back to the book of Genesis where it says, *"male and female He created them and gave them dominion over the fish of the sea, and over the fowl of the air, and over the cattle, and over all the earth, and over every creeping thing that creeepeth upon the earth" (Genesis 1:26).* The scriptures set the bar very high for the marital relationship when it instructs the wife and husband to emulate the relationship between Christ and His Church in their marriage. If someone does not love you enough to speak to you with dignity and respect, then that person is a long way from loving you enough to die for you. When a husband brings up the submit word, the wife should say, "As unto the Lord." When a man loves his wife like Christ loves His Church, submission is a lot easier to achieve. I must admit though that there are some women who are rebellious and want nothing more than to dominate their husbands, like Jezebel dominated Ahab, and that is just as pathetic as the husband who mistreats his wife but expects her to submit to his godzilla-like tactics. When a husband and wife follow the instructions in the Bible on how they should treat each other, their marriage will overcome obstacles and blossom. When the Bible blueprint on how husbands and wives are to treat each other is followed, the divorce rate in the church will not exceed the divorce rate of the world.

I remember years ago when I was asked to be the best man at a friends wedding. I told the bride and the groom that as long as Jesus is in the marriage, the marriage will be worth being in.

Looking back, it is easy to say this now, but I had no clue about the admonition from the scripture on how I should treat my wife. I wanted submission, but the expression of love and the "as unto the Lord" part of the equation was missing from the way I treated my wife. I was full of demons back then and cared only about pleasing my flesh. Unfortunately my wife, children, and others suffered the collateral damage from my reckless lifestyle. I wasn't physically abusive, but I know that I put my wife through a great deal of torment because I was tormented by devils. Sleeping with the devil can't be fun; if a man is under the control of devils, then his wife will suffer the brunt of the manifestation of those devils. I know this to be true because I was full of them and saw the toll it took on my wife.

There are times when I think about the horrible ways I treated my wife, and it leads me to weep. I constantly ask the Lord to allow me to be a blessing to her on a daily basis. I know I can't undo what was done in terms of the neglect, but going forward I can endeavor to be the best husband I can as unto the Lord. I am committed to doing this because she never gave up on me, although she had plenty of reasons to do so. She never stopped praying and interceding on my behalf, and as I look back, I can honestly say once again that the reason I am here writing this book instead of being in prison or dead is because somebody prayed for me, had me on their mind, took their time, and prayed for me. I thank the Lord Jesus for my wife for life and all the intercessors whom he has placed in my life. They didn't just pray; they also turned down their plates because my case was a tough one.

I want to encourage you today; if you have someone in prison, on drugs, or trapped in some form of bondage, please don't give up, and never stop praying and fasting because, *"The effectual fervent prayer of a righteous man availeth much" (James 5:16b).* The first thing you want to pray for is the turning of the person's mental captivity. It makes no sense to expect God to let someone out of prison so they can commit more crimes. Ask God to break the power of sin off them, then petition Him to open the door and set them free. Along with prayer, it is wise to do some fasting also, depending on the severity of the situation.

Persistent prayer pays off, so be persistent and above all else, please have faith. The Bible is replete with examples of individuals who prayed day and night until they received the breakthrough. One example is found in the book of Acts, and it involves the Apostle Peter. It was during the days of unleavened bread when Herod vexed the church by killing James, the brother of John, and arrested Peter. The Bible says Peter was kept in prison, but I love what Acts 12 verse 5 declares: *"But prayer was made without ceasing of the church unto God for him."* We are the church, and when we pray, God will open closed doors. On the night that Herod decided to send for Peter, The Bible declares he was sleeping between two soldiers, bound with two chains. Two is the number of witness and separation. Because of the prayers of the intercessors, God was about to separate Peter from the prison. The angel of the Lord came into the prison and shined a light. Someone said, "the angel freed Peter from prison but prayer summoned the angel." Persistent prayer without ceasing will bring angels into a dark situation and cause light to shine. The angelic visitation caused Peter's chains to fall off. Keep praying, beloved, because your prayers will summon angels and break chains. Hallelujah!!!

When they came to the Iron Gate that led to the city, the Bible says the gate "opened to them of its own accord." Jesus declared, *"The gates of hell will not prevail against His church."* Persistent prayer will cause iron gates to open so the captive can be set free. Iron is symbolic of strength, affliction, and judgment. Gate is symbolic of entrance, power, and authority. Here is the revelation; it does not matter how strong or how much power and authority a demon may have in afflicting us or our loved one; persistent prayer can summon angels who are stronger and have more authority.

"And when he had considered the thing, he came to the house of Mary the mother of John, whose surname was Mark; where many were gathered together praying" (Acts 12:12). When we gather together to pray, we must do so with unity. We do not need people praying who are trying to impress others by how well and how long they can pray. We need people who are dead to the flesh, people who recognize that we know not how to pray, and we need the Holy Ghost to make intercession for us because He knows the mind of Christ. Let me share something amazing with you. When Peter knocked on the gate, a young girl named Rhoda came to the door but did not let him in because upon recognizing his voice, she ran back with gladness to tell the others that he was at the gate. Beloved, when the answerer to your prayers is at the door, there is nothing wrong with gladness, but please, open the door and receive the answer!

There is something more bizarre than the fact that she did not open the door for Peter. When she ran back and told the others that Peter stood at the gate, they told her she was mad. People might think you are crazy for praying for that situation after so many years, but God will honor your fervency. The young lady's name is Rhoda, and I love the fact that she did not give up when they said she was mad. The Bible says, *"but she constantly affirmed that it was even so'"* *(12:15b)*. Despite her constant affirmation, they still did not believe it was Peter; they thought it was his angel.

They were praying but never accepted the answer when it came. Quite often we are busy going through the ritual even though the answer has already arrived. If you pray for rain, do not leave your house without your umbrella. Think. Singles, how many times have you prayed for a partner and God sent that godly person but you failed to recognize him or her? Bread winners, how many times have you prayed for more finances? God answered you in terms of a business idea, but you rejected it.

The people praying for Peter should have prayed and rejoiced when they saw him; instead, they were astonished. Persistent prayer will keep the answer knocking even though you might not recognize • it at the present time. The answer will be there. It will not leave until you accept it or reject it.

I want to hammer home my point of being persistent even when others do not believe. I love what the Bible says next: *"But Peter continued knocking: and when they had opened the door, and saw him, they were astonished" (Acts 12:16)*. Beloved, you have got to keep knocking because when they see your loved one released from prison, from drug addiction, from homosexuality, they are going to be astonished.

Please allow me to give you another example of how prayer can open the prison door. This example is also from the book of Acts, and it involves the Apostle Paul and Silas. *"And it came to pass, as we went to prayer, a certain damsel possessed with a spirit of divination met us, which brought her masters much gain by soothsaying" (Acts 16:16)*. Notice the scripture does not say, as we went to the buffet, or as we sat before our favorite television program. Jesus and the Apostles had an active prayer life. The young woman had a spirit of divination that brought a lot of money to her masters. She followed Paul and Silas around for days crying out that they were servants of the Most High God, which came to show them the way of salvation. What she said was not a bad thing, but the fact that she operated in a spirit of divination grieved Paul so much that he said, *"I command thee in the name of Jesus Christ to come out of her. And he came out the same hour"* *(Acts 16:18).* Notice Paul did not mention anything about the blood of Jesus. When her masters saw that their cash cow was gone, they incited a riot against Paul and Silas, who were severely beaten by the crowd and thrown in jail. The jailer wanted to make sure they did not escape, so he threw them into the inner prison and placed their feet in stocks. Please read this very carefully. Paul and Silas did not murmur or complain. The Bible says, *"and at midnight Paul and Silas prayed, and sang praises unto God: and the prisoners heard them.* I am belaboring this point because of its importance. Midnight represents the darkest point of the present day, but it is also the earliest point of the day. If you are willing to pray and praise in the midnight hour, some prisoners will hear you. Paul and Silas had a prayer and praise celebration in the jail that caused a sudden earthquake to shake the foundations of the prison: The Bible says, *"And immediately all the doors were opened and every one's bands were loosed"* *(Acts 16:26b).* Hallelujah, Glory to God! Why don't you take a moment right now and pray for a family member or friend who is in prison or trapped in sin. After praying, give God some praise for the answer.

If you are the family member, and you are reading this from a prison cell, and you are not saved, please take this time to ask Jesus to forgive you of your sins. Ask Him to come into your heart and be the Lord of your life. Ask Him to forgive you for all the people you hurt when you were on the streets robbing, cheating, killing, stealing, selling or using drugs, or doing both. You might not have used or dealt drugs, but you know in your heart you did other horrible things; just ask Him to forgive you and He will. You might not be in a literal prison, but you may be in a prison of pornography, homosexuality, pedophilia, or some other form of sexual perversion. Cry out to Him and He will answer you. Whatever the sin, the Blood of Jesus is sufficient to cleanse you, but you must call on Him.

I was invited to share my testimony at a youth outreach the other day, and I told a friend that twelve step programs are not bad, but the first step every sinner needs to take is the step of repentance. The journey of a thousand miles begins with the first step. When you take the first step to Jesus, He will help you navigate through the rest of the journey.

The prayers of my wife, sister, and the others broke through and opened the door to salvation, and then they opened the prison door for me. Before the prison door opened, God had a lesson for me to learn, and I was eager to learn it. I knew that when I learned it, He would give me a "suddenly" and an "immediately," as He did for Paul and Silas.

I was caught red handed but decided to take my chance at trial; in retrospect, I should have pled guilty and accepted my punishment. My friend had converted to Islam and threw himself into the Koran, but I was not interested. I knew I needed a spiritual awakening, but in my heart I did not believe Islam was the way. I did not know much about the God to whom my grandmother prayed, but I remembered her zeal and dedication to her God. Thank God for praying grandparents. I had a great deal of time on my hand, so I spent most of it exercising and reading newspapers and magazines. Remand would last about a year, and it was very claustrophobic being locked in a small cell for a long period of time.

I went from Wormwood Scrubs to Brixton Prison, then to some other places where I awaited trial. I had very few visits because the majority of my family was in America. I read voraciously and exercised as much as I could to keep my mind from falling into a state of depression. For some reason, the weather always seemed gloomy and overcast. I always wondered whether that was the reason why there were so many pubs (bars) in England. I was surrounded by inmates who drank and got high when they could. I knew that it was my lifestyle of drinking and drug dealing that had led me to prison, and I wanted nothing to do with either. Some people go to prison and immerse themselves into a life of crime right in prison, but I made the decision to better myself while I was there.

The Gideon Bible society is famous for leaving Bibles in hotels, prisons, and other places. I found a small New Testament in the cell and began reading it. Before incarceration, the extent of my Bible reading had been the few Psalms I'd read. I was deceived into thinking I could get protection from the Psalms but would not humble myself and serve the one of whom the Psalmists wrote. It makes no sense to me to read a manual and refuse to follow the instructions of that manual. I met some Rastafarians while in prison, and they called on the name of Emperor Haile Selassie I of Ethiopia. I guess they figured that if they were going to pray to a man, then that man had to be from Africa—not a long-haired white man hanging on a cross. The thing I could never figure out was, the same Bible that speaks about Jesus is the Bible they were reading, but they refused to acknowledge Him. I told them I would not waste my time reading a book, which I thought had been tampered with.

I was reading the Bible, and although I was in a spiritually confused state, I was intrigued by some of the things written in it. I kept thinking about my grandmother's dedication to her God; I knew she was a devout Christian, but I was blinded by bigotry because of the racism I had suffered coming from Jamaica to the United States. The white kids used to tell us to go back to Africa, and that was kind of comical because I had never been to Africa. The only images on TV about Africa were from the Tarzan movies, which portrayed the Africans in a very negative light. My response to the white kids was, "Give me back all the riches your people stole from Africa first." I categorically rejected Christianity because I could not get past the picture of the long-haired white man on the cross. As far as I was concerned, it was a white man's religion. I felt that European missionaries went to Africa with the Bible, then took over the lands of the Africans while turning their culture upside down. I studied history, and I was incensed about the treatment of the American Indians on their own land. Because of colonialism and the domination of different cultures all around the globe, I thought the white man was the devil. I did not think about the fact that the Africans who sold their people were also to blame, and so were Muslim Arabs, who were in the interior of Africa getting wealthy off the slave trade. When the mini-series Roots came out, I was really ticked off about what happened to Kunta Kinte. My heart needed a transformation, and I was rejecting the very one who had the power to transform it. Although I was reading the little Gideon Bible on a regular basis, I had no true concept of the real Jesus—but I was about to learn.

Racism filled me with a lot of bitterness and anger before I was arrested in England, and I fed my soul with a great deal of Black

Nationalist Teachings. I could not rationalize in my mind why people hated me because of the color of my skin. I looked at the apartheid system in South Africa as the ultimate injustice. There was no country in Europe where a black man had control and oppressed the white population. I looked at the life of the honorable Nelson Mandela, a freedom fighter who was jailed for many years because he wanted to see his homeland free from oppression. I looked at the poor people of South Africa living in Bantustans—land set aside by the Apartheid regime. I liked the speaking ability of Dr. Martin Luther King Jr. but had little regard for his non-violent philosophy, especially when I saw videos of black people being sprayed with water that shot out of the hose like a ball out of a cannon; especially when I saw black people being bitten by dogs just because they wanted to be treated with dignity. I began to listen to a lot of Malcolm X tapes, and adopted the slogan of Marcus Garvey and the Universal Negro Improvement Association movement. With that type of mind set, you can see why I wanted nothing to do with the Eurocentric form of Christianity or the religion of Muslim Arabs whose forefathers were complicit in the oppression of Africans. Besides the oppression in South Africa, I kept hearing there were black people who were enslaved in parts of Africa like the Sudan.

Jesus, angels, and all Biblical characters in the majority of the Christian books and Bibles had pictures that were white, and I was having none off that. I used to shake my head when I went into certain churches and even some black peoples' homes and saw the picture of the white man hanging on the wall. I felt they were brainwashed and totally deceived. Matters were exacerbated by the fact that everything black was described as evil. Racism is a sin, whether or not it is being perpetrated by whites or blacks, but as far as I was concerned, I had a right to be angry because my anger and hatred was in response to the racial injustice I'd suffered along with other blacks.

It is probably very difficult for a white person to understand the stigma with which black people have to live because of the history of racial abuse. I saw a round table discussion on TV one day, and one of the speakers had a response for people who say black people like to use the race card. He asked a question that I will never forget. He said, "How did the card get in the deck?" Once the card is in the deck, it is going to be a part of the game. The card is still in the deck because, despite the fact that the United States has come a long way on race relations, there is still institutionalized racism in this country. Until it is eliminated in its entirety, blacks and whites will have to work together to see that it is eliminated.

The prison was a captive place where God got my attention long enough to deal with the quagmire of bitterness, which permeated my soul. I didn't know it at the time, but the little Gideon Bible was the instrument God would use to deliver me. Before I delve fully into the manner in which the Lord transformed my life through his word, I want to take a look at the agent God used to cleanse my sin. That agent is the Blood of Jesus, and I found out that it is the only thing that can wash away the stench and stain of sin.

CHAPTER 6

There is Power in the Blood

September 11, 2001 was a watershed moment in the history of America. It was the day radical Muslim fundamentalists hijacked our airplanes and unleashed a wave of death and destruction that is still reverberating in our society. Many of these fundamentalists are trying to destroy America because they blame us for backing Israel and because they believe that Jews and Christians are infidels. The seed of this conflict was sown the day Ishmael began to torment Isaac. It continues to play out in the Middle East as the descendants of Isaac and the descendants of Ishmael wage war for the lands in the Middle East. For many years, the United States and countries in Western Europe were left unscathed in the battle, although they have influenced the socio-economic and the geo-political climate of the Middle East. All of that changed on September 11, 2001.

I believe every American can tell you exactly where they were when they heard the news of airplanes crashing into the World Trade Center. I was at the daycare of the church I attended. The memory is so vivid it might as well be yesterday. The daycare director called my attention to the news flash coming from the television. The news anchor was reporting that a plane had just crashed into the World Trade Center. I watched in horror as flames engulfed the towers. While trying to come to terms with the tragic events unfolding, another plane flew into the other tower. I knew immediately that the nation was under attack, and life as I knew it had changed forever.

While watching the horrific scene unfold, I received a call from my sister Nena. She informed me that our sister Janet worked in one of the towers. At that very moment, the tragedy hit home and became more personal than ever. There is a tendency to become desensitized and detached because of all the murder and mayhem we watch and listen to on the evening news. We see graphic images of people being blown up and gunned down. We feel a sense of remorse but also a sense of detachment when we do not know the victim or victims. When the victim is a loved one, words cannot describe the utter distress and helplessness that is felt, but words will have to suffice. Once I found out that my sister might be in one of the buildings, I left the daycare immediately and headed home. I remember praying to the Lord for mercy—not only for Janet but also for every other person in the building and for the many families affected by the tragedy. That afternoon, I received word that Janet had made it out of the towering inferno, and I was grateful yet saddened by the great loss of other families. When I spoke with Janet, she told me that she's felt the building shake and saw a crack in the wall and knew she was in danger. She explained that she fled the building, and when she made it outside, she found the area blanketed by a thick cloud of ash, which made breathing difficult, and at one point sought refuge under an ambulance. The atmosphere was so thick with the ash that Janet could not see. She heard a voice while she was under the ambulance, saying, "Open the door and let people in." Thinking the ambulance was about to pull off with her under it, she reached out and was pulled inside. She told me the thing that kept her going was a message she remembered ministering called the Blood of Jesus. She kept saying, "The Blood of Jesus, The Blood of Jesus, The Blood of Jesus." Mercy and Grace allows us to escape divine judgment in order to receive salvation.

Faith is the vehicle that carries us to salvation. Now we come to the cleansing agent used by God to cleanse us of our sins to facilitate salvation. This agent is the Blood of Jesus Christ, the Lamb of God. One of the first things a doctor will do to determine what is ailing a sick individual is to order blood work. Blood work not only identifies what is attacking our system but also helps the doctor to rule out other illnesses. God said He has given us the blood to make atonement for our souls: For it is the blood that makes atonement for the soul. The Hebrew word for atonement is *Kawfar*, and it means *to cover, to expiate, or to cancel.* It also means *to cleanse, to disannul, or to be merciful.* I like the definition that was given to me by one of my Bible professors and mentors, Dr. Lillian Ferguson. Dr. Ferguson said, "Atonement is when two individuals or entities that have been separated are brought back together as one." We have already established the fact that the soul is the seat of the human will, intellect, and emotion. Let us go deeper into this concept. Genesis 2:7 states, *"And the Lord God formed man of the dust of the ground, and breathed into his nostrils the breath of life; and man became a living soul."* The Hebrew word for soul is *Nehfesh*, and it means, *to breathe, to be breathed upon, or refreshed (as if by a current of air).* God breathed the breath of life into man, and he in turn began to breathe, think, and to feel. Meditate for a moment on the fact that blood carries the air we breathe to the body so life can be sustained. If an individual's blood is contaminated, the contamination is carried throughout the body by the blood.

Adam's sin caused a breach in the relationship between him and God. The breach made an altar of sacrifice necessary for atonement. Dr. Sproul writes, *"For those who have tasted the sweetness of the forgiveness of and reconciliation with God, His ubiquity is good news. But for those who remain hostile and estranged from God, His omnipresence is very bad news. There is nothing a fugitive wants to hear less than that his pursuer is everywhere. There is no place to hide from an infinite spirit. His eye is on the sparrow when it falls. His eye is also on the thief when he steals. There are those who hate God's presence because they cannot stand His gaze. But for those who love His appearing, the presence of God is like soothing music."*

After telling the reader that all human beings have sinned and come short of God's glory, the Apostle Paul then tells the reader the result of sin and the gift God has provided. In Romans 6:23, he writes, *"the wages of sin is death: but the gift of God is eternal life through Jesus Christ our Lord."* Before we examine the gift, its relation to the blood sacrifice, and how God has provided it, let us examine the origin of sin and how it has affected all human beings. The book of Genesis is a book of beginnings. In the book, we find the description of the beginning of the earth, the creation of man and woman, and their placement in a beautiful garden by God. Genesis 2:15–17 states, *"And the LORD God took the man, and put him into the Garden of Eden to dress it and to keep it. And the LORD God commanded the man, saying, Of every tree of the garden thou mayest freely eat: But of the tree of the knowledge of good and evil, thou shalt not eat of it: for in the day that thou eatest thereof thou shalt surely die."* It is worth noting that the knowledge of evil is in the garden with the knowledge of good. The reader might ask why the knowledge of evil was in the garden with the knowledge of good. The author's answer is that it is there for God's divine purpose, and that purpose will be revealed to us when we meet God. Isaiah 45:5–7 states, *"I am the LORD, and there is none else, there is no God beside me: I girded thee, though thou hast not known me: That they may know from the rising of the sun, and from the west, that there is none beside me. I am the LORD, and there is none else. I form the light, and create darkness: I make peace, and create evil: I the LORD do all these things."* Was the knowledge of evil in the garden to test the free will God had given to Adam? That is a possibility. At a point of time unknown to us, that free will was tested, and the result led to catastrophic consequences. Genesis 3:1 states, *"Now the serpent was more subtle than any beast of the field which the Lord God had made. And he said unto the woman, yea, has God said, you shall not eat of every tree of the garden?"* The word subtle in the Hebrew is *awroom*, and it means *cunning [usually in a bad way] or crafty.* The serpent probes the woman to discern her knowledge of the commandment of the Lord. A probe is sent to gather information in order to determine the best way to attack. The serpent was looking for an opening, and the woman's response provided one. It is important to point out that the creature that conversed with the woman did not look like a snake at that point, although it had the subtlety and the craftiness of one. Gene Cunningham writes, *"The Hebrew word for serpent is* nachash, *and it means 'the shining one.' Not until after the fall did God curse the serpent and it became a symbol of sin. In Revelation 12:9 the serpent is identified as the devil, Satan, the one who deceives the world."* Genesis 3:2–3 gives us Eve's response: *"And the woman said unto the serpent, we may eat of the fruit of the trees of the garden: But of the fruit of the tree which is in the midst of the garden, God has said, you shall not eat of it, neither shall you touch It, lest you die."*

To her credit, the woman attempts to defend the Word of God, but unfortunately she misquotes Him. God did not tell them they could not touch the fruit. He told them they could not eat it. Ignorance of God's word was the opening the adversary was looking for, and he wasted no time in attacking that weakness. When he first comes to the woman he is asking a question, but once he gets his answer, he makes an emphatic statement. Genesis 3:4-5: *"And the serpent said unto the woman, you shall not surely die: For God does know that in the day you eat thereof, then your eyes shall be opened, and you shall be as gods, knowing good and evil" (Genesis 3:4-5).*

He entices the woman with a partial truth. Her eyes would be open once she ate of the tree, but the serpent did not tell her what she would see. He led her to believe that she would be like God. There is nothing wrong with wanting to be like God in terms of having Godly characteristics, but the serpent's idea of being like God is actually a perverted desire to receive the honor and worship due to God alone. Isaiah backs up this assertion in chapter 14:12–16. The prophet wrote, *"How art thou fallen from heaven, O Lucifer, son of the morning! How art thou cut down to the ground, which didst weaken the nations! For thou hast said in thine heart, I will ascend into heaven, I will exalt my throne above the stars of God: I will sit also upon the mount of the congregation, in the sides of the north: I will ascend above the heights of the clouds; I will be like the most High. Yet thou shalt be brought down to hell, to the sides of the pit. They that see thee shall narrowly look upon thee, and consider thee, saying, Is this the man that made the earth to tremble, that did shake kingdoms; That made the world as a wilderness, and destroyed the cities thereof; that opened not the house of his prisoners?"* He knew first hand the result of rebelling against God's word. Cunningham writes, *"He knows that Eve is thinking in terms of physical death. He also knows that she will not fall down and die physically the instant she eats from the tree, so his words are half true. God's warning in Genesis 2:17 uses the Hebrew word for death, muth, twice: 'In the day you eat of this tree, dying you shall surely die.' God was telling them that they would eventually die physically."*

The question one has to ask is this: How can we become like God by disobeying God? Adam and Eve found out the answer to that question. Genesis 3:6–7: *"And when the woman saw that the tree was good for food, and that it was pleasant to the eyes, and a tree to be desired to make one wise, she took of the fruit thereof, and did eat, and gave also unto her husband with her; and he did eat. And the eyes of them both were opened, and they knew that they were naked; and they sewed fig leaves together, and made themselves aprons."* It is a sad indictment on Adam that he did not intervene when the serpent was conversing with his wife. He was placed in the garden to have dominion, and at a crucial moment, he was missing in action. There are many men who are missing in spiritual action, and their homes are left uncovered. When Adam appears, he is disobeying the commandment of God and transferring dominion to the devil. The Bible says they hear the voice of the Lord God walking in the garden in the cool of the day: and Adam and his wife hid themselves from the presence of the Lord God amongst the trees of the garden. I guess they figured that since they had fig leaves on, they could blend in with the trees. When God confronts him with the rhetorical question, "Adam where art thou?" he explains to God that he heard His voice, in the garden and was afraid because he was naked, so he hid himself. Sinners have been attempting to hide from God ever since. When tragedy strikes, the first thing they ask is, "Why did God allow it to happen?" God is omniscient, so He is not ignorant of their location. He is giving Adam a chance to confess and acknowledge his condition before Him.

Instead of confessing his sin and falling on the mercies of God, Adam and Eve play what I call the blame game. When God asked him who told him that he was naked, and whether he'd eaten from the forbidden tree, Adam tells God, *"The woman whom thou gavest to be with me, she gave me of the tree, and I did eat" (Genesis 3:12).* He was speaking the truth, but he neglected to mention the fact that he had dropped the ball by not protecting his wife from the serpent. It is ironic that when he first saw Eve, his response was, *"this is now bone of my bones, and flesh of my flesh" (Genesis 2:23).* When tragedy strikes, she is the woman God gave to him. He does not mention the fact that he had dominion and should have protected her from the deceptive serpent. When Eve is confronted, she says, *"the serpent beguiled me, and I did eat"* (Genesis 3:13). She spoke the truth also, but God did not ask her what the serpent did, He asked her what *she* did. Their attempt to cover themselves with an apron made of fig leaves is man's first attempt to expiate his sin through a covering. Today we see men and women trying to cover their nakedness with everything but what God has provided. From very early on, God showed us that the shedding of blood would be the method used to cleanse mankind of sin. He also tells us who would provide the blood. Gen. 3:21 says, *"Unto Adam also and to his wife did the LORD God make coats of skins, and clothed them."* In Genesis 3:15, we have what is called the *proto evangel*. The *proto evangel* is the first mention of God's plan to defeat the enemy through the seed of the woman and bring forth restoration. In speaking to the serpent, God said, *"And I will put enmity between thee and the woman, and between thy seed and her seed; it shall bruise thy head, and thou shalt bruise his heel."* From this passage, we understand that the deliverer would come from the seed of a woman.

God is truly a God of restoration. Sin entered the world because she was deceived, but God would bring forth the promised seed through a woman. The calling of Abram by God is a watershed event in the Bible. God called him from the land of Ur of the Chaldees. Abram was seventy-five when the Lord called him; his wife Sarai was sixty-five. Abram's obedience to the call of God is astounding when you consider the fact that God asked him to leave all that was familiar to go to a land that He would show him. His obedience is the primary reason he is called the father of the faithful. If a seventy-five-year-old man and his sixty-five-year-old wife can do it, no one has an excuse.

God promised him that he would have a son. In an attempt to expedite the process, Sarai convinced Abram to sleep with her maid, Hagar. Hagar bears him a son, whom he named Ishmael. The Lord next appears to Abram when he is ninety years old and promises to make a covenant with him. It is at this time that the Lord changes his name to Abraham. The name Abraham means "father of many nations," and it is symbolic of the promise from God to make his descendants innumerable like the sand on the seashore. His wife's name was changed to Sarah, which means "mother of nations." Sarah conceived and bore Abraham a son when he was a hundred years old, and he named him Isaac. At a certain point in time, Abraham is given the test of a lifetime by God.

"And it came to pass after these things that God did tempt Abraham, and said unto him, Abraham: and he said, Behold, here I am. And he said, Take now thy son, thine only son Isaac, whom thou lovest, and get thee into the land of Moriah; and offer him there for a burnt offering upon one of the mountains which I will tell thee of" (Gen 22:1–2).

When they arrive at Mount Moriah, Isaac asked his dad where the sacrifice was. Abram's answer paints a portrait for us of how to trust God. He told Isaac, *"God will provide himself a lamb for a burnt offering" (Genesis 22:8a).* I like to interpret this as, God the Son would offer himself as the Paschal Lamb. The word "tempt" in Hebrew is not used in the same way as we use it in English. The Hebrew word for tempt is *nawsaw,* and it means, *to test, or to prove.* In this particular verse, Abraham is a type of a father willing to sacrifice his beloved son. The word "type" means, "a class, group, or category of things or persons sharing one or more characteristics." Isaac is a type of the savior because he is a promised seed. Abraham saw Mount Moriah on the third day. Three is a number that represents resurrection and increase. The Savior would be the way, the truth, and the life, He would be crucified the third hour, but He would rise on the third day. The word *Moriah* means, "Chosen by God," and it represents a place and time when God will call upon every individual.

The purpose of the call will be to test us to determine if there is anything in our lives so dear that we are unwilling to lay it on the altar of sacrifice. The time and the place of that sacrifice will not be one of convenience for us, but for God. Abraham called the name of the place Jehovah Jireh, which means, "The Lord will provide." I like to give it the definition, "the provision of the Lord will be seen." Abraham's willingness to obey the command of God to sacrifice his beloved son Isaac elicits a powerful response from God. Because of his willingness and his obedience, the Lord said to him, *"in blessing I will bless you, and in multiplying I will multiply your seed as the stars of the heaven and as the sand which is upon the sea shore; and thy seed shall possess the gate of his enemies. In thy seed shall all the nations of the earth be blessed; because thou hast obeyed my voice" (Genesis 22:17-18).*

Beloved, no matter what the situation or circumstance we may face, let us endeavor to obey the still, small voice of God. Inherent in His still, small voice is the blessing we need to give us peace, comfort, and deliverance from our troubles. Isaac eventually has two sons named Esau and Jacob. Joseph was one of the twelve sons of Jacob, whose name was changed to Israel.

The Bible says a new king arose, which knew not Joseph, and he was jealous of the abundance and prosperity of the children of Israel and ordered taskmasters to afflict them. This constitutes the fulfillment of the prophecy given to Abram by God concerning his descendants being afflicted in a strange land. In the fullness of time, the Lord raised up a deliverer named Moses. He was an Israelite who grew up in the house of Pharaoh. Moses was raised up by God to deliver the Israelites out of bondage and establish a sacrificial system that would enable the people to receive pardon for their transgressions. Now that we have looked at a very brief history of the period between Abraham and Moses, let us examine the establishment of the sacrifices instituted by God. Keep in mind that these sacrifices would be a type and a shadow of the ultimate sacrifice, which would be made by the promised seed. When God was ready to deliver His people from the bondage of Egypt, He gave His servant Moses explicit instructions on how the people should prepare. God told Moses that the only way the death angel would pass a house is if blood was on the two side posts and on the upper doorpost of the house, over the door. The blood had to be from a lamb without spot or blemish. Egypt was a place of bondage, and deliverance was instituted by the shedding of the blood of a lamb without blemish.

After God delivered the people with a mighty hand, He instructed Moses to ordain his brother Aaron as the high priest. Aaron would minister before Him in order to obtain atonement for the sins of the people via sacrificial offerings. *"And if his offering be of the flocks, namely, of the sheep, or of the goats, for a burnt sacrifice; he shall bring it a male without blemish"* (Leviticus 1:10). The Lord instituted five offerings for the altar of sacrifice, because five is the number in scripture that represents grace. We are saved by grace through faith.

1) *The burnt offering*: This is the premier offering given on the altar of sacrifice. The priests would keep the skin and everything else had to be burned, with only the ashes remaining. The priests receiving the skin paint a wonderful picture of the covering God made

86

for Adam and Eve out of animal's skin. 2) *The peace offering*: The promised seed would restore peace between God and man. 3) *The sin offering*: The promised seed is seen here as the substitute for us. 4) *The trespass offering*: This offering was two-fold in that it covered trespasses against God and our neighbors. 5) *The meat offering*: This typifies the humanity of the promised seed. It is only through the shedding of blood that we have remission of sins. *"And almost all things are by the law purged with blood; and without shedding of blood is no remission" (Hebrews 9:22).* This is the key component, which separates Christianity from all other faiths. There can be no remission of sin without the shedding of blood.

As I mentioned earlier, God's institution of the blood sacrifice as recorded in the book of Leviticus was a shadow and a type of a larger plan of salvation. In order to access salvation, the sinner needs to repent of his sins so the blood of Jesus can cleanse him. In order to manifest this plan, God would have to bring forth the promised seed of the woman, because the high priest who entered into the holy of holies with blood would have to offer a sacrifice for his own sins first. The seed of the woman would be sinless so he would be able to offer himself a sacrifice once and for all. He would have no need to offer any sacrifices for himself because he would be the Lamb without a blemish.

In the fullness of time, the Lord sent His angel Gabriel to a virgin espoused to a man named Joseph. *"And in the sixth month the angel Gabriel was sent from God unto a city of Galilee, named Nazareth, to a virgin espoused to a man whose name was Joseph, of the house of David; and the virgin's name was Mary. And the angel came in unto her, and said, Hail, thou that art highly favored, the Lord is with thee: blessed art thou among women. And when she saw him, she was troubled at his saying, and cast in her mind what manner of salutation this should be. And the angel said unto her, 'Fear not, Mary: for thou hast found favor with God. And, behold, thou shalt conceive in thy womb, and bring forth a son, and shalt call his name JESUS. He shall be great, and shall be called the Son of the Highest: and the Lord God shall give unto him the throne of his father David: And he shall reign over the house of Jacob for ever; and of his kingdom there shall be no end.' Then said Mary unto the angel, 'how shall this be, seeing I know not a man?' And* the angel answered and said unto her, 'The Holy Ghost shall come upon thee, and the power of the Highest shall overshadow thee: therefore also that holy thing which shall be born of thee shall be called the Son of God" (Luke 1: 26-35).

What a wonderful fulfillment of the promise of a seed. He would be great, He would be the Son of the Most High, and His kingdom would have no end. The reason why He had to be the seed of a woman was because God would be his Father. Like the lamb without blemish, He could not have the sinful nature of an earthly father, because He could not be the propitiation for our sins if He had a sin nature. Although He was born to be King, his first crib was a manger in a stable of animals. In the natural, it does not seem like a proper entrance into the world for one who would be the Son of the Most High, but God has chosen the foolish things of this world to confound the wise. His humble birthplace is a testament to the fact that He can identify with human beings trapped in situations that make them live like animals.

When it was time for His public ministry, He came to the Jordan, where his cousin John the Baptist was baptizing people. The religious leaders sent priests and Levites to ask John who he was. John's response when he saw Jesus is an awesome confirmation and fulfillment of the salvation God promised to mankind. *"And they asked him, and said unto him, Why baptizest thou then, if thou be not that Christ, nor Elias, neither that prophet? John answered them, saying, I baptize with water: but there standeth one among you, whom ye know not; He it is, who coming after me is preferred before me, whose shoe's latchet I am not worthy to unloose. These things were done in Bethabara beyond Jordan, where John was baptizing. The next day John seeth Jesus coming unto him, and saith, **Behold the Lamb of God, which taketh away the sin of the world.** This is he of whom I said, After me cometh a man which is preferred before me: for he was before me. And I knew him not: but that he should be made manifest to Israel, therefore am I come baptizing with water. And John bare record, saying, I saw the Spirit descending from heaven like a dove, and it abode upon him. And I knew him not: but he that sent me to baptize with water, the same said unto me, Upon whom thou shalt see the Spirit descending, and remaining on him, the same is he which* *baptizeth with the Holy Ghost. And I saw, and bare record that this is the Son of God" (John 1:25-34).*

God fulfilled His promise to provide a seed by sending His only begotten son to die on the cross. His heel was bruised when He was crucified, but He bruised the serpent's head when He arose triumphantly on the third day, and took the keys of death, hell, and the grave from Satan. Because of His death, burial, and resurrection, men and women no longer have to suffer the torments of the devil and his minions. They can believe in the Lord Jesus and receive freedom from the power and the penalty of sin. Hallelujah! Jesus shed His blood not only to provide salvation but also to start us on a journey of sanctification and glorification. Salvation is the beginning of the journey, not the end of it. Many people receive salvation and don't press on to know the Lord intimately. He has so much more for us than simply escaping the wrath to come. He wants to bring us to a place of perfection. The perfecting process will come to fruition through the church He is building. The first step to that process is coming to the realization that a sinner cannot live in the flesh and expect be in right standing with God.

We must understand there is nothing good in the flesh because it is the center of all that is carnal and wicked in a man. As foresaid, I don't care what religious background a person comes from—I don't care if the person has any religious background at all. We all have to deal with the struggle within. An individual can have all the wealth at his disposal; he could be a product of the finest educational institutions and be brought up with proper etiquette. He still has to fight the urge to be overcome by sin. Why do you think some of the most serious crimes are committed by people with wealth and prestige? It is because those people have more opportunities to fall into sin.

When my world came crashing in on that cold November night in London, I knew that my sinful lifestyle was the cause of that crash. I was not going to use excuses, such as my parents were separated when I was a child, and I couldn't do better because I was the victim of racism, or I had a rough upbringing. Sure, there were some rough days growing up, but I had it better than a lot of people. I received repeated warnings concerning where my lifestyle would lead me.

If true change is going to come to you, then you must be willing to take responsibility for the decisions that you made, decisions that have left you in the place where you are. You might be the victim of some horrific act, but at some point you have to make up your mind to move forward. You have grown men and women that are still carrying scars from things that happened to them when they were children. At some point, you will have to build a bridge and get over it because you will not make forward progress if you are constantly looking behind.

The Apostle Paul told the Philippians, *"Brethren, I count not myself to have apprehended: but this one thing I do, forgetting those things which are behind, and reaching forth unto those things which are before, I press toward the mark for the prize of the high calling of God in Christ Jesus" (Philippians 3: 13-14).* In Bible terminology, to forget does not mean to fail to remember. It means no longer being influenced or affected by something. If you are going to attain the mark of the prize of the high calling, then you will have to make up your mind to refuse to be negatively influenced or affected by your past. If anything, you should use past incidents as motivation. When life throws you a stumbling block, then make it a stepping stone. When you experience a set back, do not take a step back, because God is working on your comeback. I had to come to that realization as I sat in the cold prison cell with the prospect of many years in prison before me. I couldn't lament about the past. Yesterday had gone into eternity; tomorrow was not promised; today is a gift, and that is why it is called the present. It was time to be responsible for the mess I had made of my life. Fortunately for me, God was about to give me a message out of my mess, and a ministry out of my misery. The epiphany would come on March 6, 1991 as I read the little Gideon New Testament. When an individual is truly converted, it is a day and a time he will never forget because it is life transforming.

CHAPTER 7

Set Free in Prison

The Word of God is absolutely amazing in its ability to give new revelation and insight when you read it, and open your heart to receive from the wisdom it contains. In my opinion, there is no other book in the world like it. You can read a chapter and a verse a hundred times and on the hundredth and first time, God will give you new revelation by illuminating that chapter or verse. The Word of God is like a key that can open any cage of sin that has us bound, and it was about to open a cage in my life. It sounds like an oxymoron when I state that I was set free in prison, but that is exactly what happened to me. I read from Matthew to The Revelation several times, but on March 6, 1991, I had an epiphany while reading John, Chapter 5. The words in that particular book pierced my heart and set me on a course of total transformation. It wasn't the first time I'd read that chapter, but this time there was something different. This time it was a *Kairos,* or opportune moment. My transformation was so radical I have to describe it in detail.

At the time, I did not know the Holy Ghost was convicting me of sin and drawing me to Jesus. John, Chapter 5 records the healing of the lame man at the pool called Bethesda. It is called Bethesda because it has five porches. It is important to remember that the number five in scripture represents grace, and grace can be defined as God's unmerited favor or His divine enablement. Someone once described grace as getting what we did not deserve. A sinful man deserves death, but through the sacrifice of Jesus Christ, he can receive eternal life. *Be-thes-da* means *house of mercy.* Mercy can be described as not getting what we deserve. In retrospect, I now see how God's grace and mercy worked together to bring me to Jesus.

There were many people at the pool who were sick. John 5:3 states, "*In these lay a great multitude of impotent folk, of blind, halt, withered, waiting for the moving of the water. For an angel went down at a certain season into the pool, and troubled the water: whosoever then first after the troubling of the water stepped in was made whole of whatsoever disease he had.*" Verse 5 says, "*And a certain man was there which had an infirmity thirty and eight years.*" Thirty represents preparation for ministry, and eight represents new beginnings. When Jesus saw him lying there, and knew that he had been there a long time in that condition, He asked the man if he wanted to be made whole. The man wanted to give Jesus a long story, but Jesus cut to the chase and told him, "*Rise, take up thy bed, and walk.*" The Bible says the man was made whole immediately. Beloved, it does not matter how long you have been battling your current infirmity. Please do not become weary because Jesus is still troubling the water and bringing healing. If you repent of your sins and ask Him to come into your heart, he will save you and set you on course for total deliverance. You can't work your way into salvation, because Jesus has already paid the price for all sins.

Jesus came under serious persecution because He healed the man on the Sabbath. The religious zealots actually tried to kill Jesus. Jesus' response was, "*My Father has been working until now, and I have been working*" *(John 5:17 NKJV)*. The religious folks who were incensed by his response tried harder to kill Jesus. For the first time in my life, I began to hear the voice of Jesus. I came under deep conviction when I read these words: "*Then answered Jesus and said unto them, Verily, verily, I say unto you, The Son can do nothing of himself, but what he seeth the Father do: for what things so ever he doeth, these also doeth the Son likewise*" *(John 5:19)*. There was an epic struggle taking place in my soul as I pondered the claims Jesus was making about Himself. For most of my adult life, I had been a black nationalist who had espoused the teachings of Malcolm X and the Honorable Marcus Mosiah Garvey. Although my grandparents were devout Christians, I had denied Christianity, categorically, as a way of life for myself. As fore said, I could not get past the picture of the longhaired white man

I saw hanging in many homes and many churches. I always thought he could not be God because he looked like some of the white people who had chased me growing up and called me NIGGER. The "five percenters" always told me that the white man was the devil; the Muslims told me the Jews had corrupted the scriptures; and the Rastafarians told me Emperor Haile Selassie was God, and King James and Shakespeare had written the Bible. Now I was alone with the Bible and hearing the voice of the real Jesus. I believe religion has a pseudo Jesus at its center, and that is why it is so difficult for people to get delivered. When a sinner hears the voice of the real Jesus Christ, he will see the need to repent and be converted.

I knew it was the real Jesus because there was no preacher in the cell with me, no church choir, and no wife telling me I needed to give my heart to the Lord—but something was happening to me. Jesus was saying I had to accept Him to escape damnation and receive everlasting life. I remember crying out, "What does one man dying on the cross have to do with me personally?" A soft voice spoke to the depths of my soul and said, "Take every filthy sin you have ever committed and put it on Him." I knew I had done some terrible, vile acts. The voice went on to say, "Don't stop there. Take every sin committed by your mother, father, children, and put them on Him." I began to weep in my cell as thoughts of the filthy life I had lived flooded my soul. All those years of drug dealing, fornication, and adultery flashed across my mind, and I couldn't help but wonder if I could be cleansed of all that filth. There was another voice trying to convince me that I could not live for Jesus because I was in prison, and what was I going to do once I came out and no one hired me? Prison is a rough place, and I believe many people turn to Islam in prison because it allows them to fit into a group that believes in an eye for an eye, along with the fact that it is a religion of works. I ignored the contrary voice because I realized that I might not make it out of that wretched place, and if I didn't, then it would not matter if I could get a job or not. I knew at that moment that there was a Divine Presence in the cell with me, and I wanted the forgiveness and cleansing He provided. I remembered there was a part in the Gideon's Bible that told you how to ask Jesus into your heart. I knelt, turned to the page, and told Jesus I was a sinner. I told him I believed

He'd shed His blood for my sins, and I wanted Him to come into my life and be my savior. Words cannot adequately describe the peace and joy that filled my soul, but suffice it to say, my dark soul lit up with the light of the Lord Jesus. Instantly, I went from darkness into His marvelous light! The mental anguish I feared was eradicated immediately. Hallelujah!! There was a fire lit under me, and I could not wait for the cell doors to open so I could begin to be a witness for Jesus. I realized that I was a dead man who had received a pardon, and I wanted to reach other dead men to tell them that the Word became flesh and died on the cross for their sins, so they could have eternal life through Jesus Christ.

I was set free in prison; that sounds like a paradox, but if the Son sets you free you are free indeed. There are many people who have never suffered from a physical incarceration in a jail or prison, but they are bound by a stronghold of sin. There are many people in a physical jail or prison, but they have been set free by the Son of God.

Eight, the Number of New Beginnings

My first trial ended in a hung jury, and I was tried again—only this time the verdict was against me, and I was found guilty. I can still remember the day the judge handed me a sentence of eight years. I made up in my mind that whatever the sentence, I would have to handle it because I needed to be responsible for the crime I had committed. It wasn't life and it wasn't a death sentence. I sat stoically as the judge finished saying what he had to say. I remember being placed in a cage in a prison van to take the long journey to the place where I would serve my sentence. I had more time to reflect on my life and the things I had done to get to that point.

I remember when I came from court after getting sentenced to eight years. I was met by an inmate named Patrick Thomas. He asked me how it went in court, and I told him my sentence. I could see the look of sadness on his face, but I had peace because by that time Jesus had already set me free. Patrick Thomas went home on what is called home leave and was murdered in an apartment. When I heard the news from his co-defendant, I realized that it is better to be in prison with Jesus in your life than to be in the world without Him.

Patrick Thomas never got the chance to enjoy his freedom because a gunman took his life.

There were several other inmates from Swaleside and other prisons who got out, went right back to a life of crime, and were murdered shortly after their release. I had a sense deep down in my soul that if I was not locked up at that particular time, I would have died in the streets. Some of the people I'd associated with when I was on the streets died horrific deaths, or were sentenced to lengthy prison terms while I was inside. One of them was burned badly in a fire when he re-entered his home to rescue his son. He died in the hospital shortly thereafter. There was another associate who was trailed by some of the people he hustled with, taken from his car, beaten, shot, and robbed. I believe the police found his body in a park. I am sure there are people in neighborhoods all over this country who can tell horror stories of the casualties that came about as a result of the proliferation of crack cocaine in the eighties and early nineties. There are many people in prison who can tell their own stories about close calls and brushes with death. Sometimes, an individual has to be locked down to be made free. In the Christian faith, you have to be willing to die if you want to live. If you want to go up, then you must be willing to go down, and if you want to be rich, you must be willing to be poor.

The prison bars had me locked in, but I was enjoying my freedom in the Lord Jesus. Words cannot adequately describe the joy of a soul that has been set free from sin after many years of a debauched lifestyle, so I will let the Bible describe the Heavenly celebration. *"Likewise I say unto you, there is joy in the presence of the angels of God over one sinner that repenteth" (Luke 15:10).* True repentance brings a Heavenly celebration because repentance means to turn. I hear many preachers telling people to make a three hundred and sixty-degree turn, but that type of turn just puts you in a circle—you wind up where you began. A repentant person makes a one hundred and eighty-degree turn from sin to God. The conversion of a sinner from death to eternal life has to be the greatest miracle of all. When you meditate on the fact that Jesus was the Word that became flesh in order to die on the cross for the redemption of lost souls, you have to realize that you owe Him everything. I can't speak for you, the reader, but I know that I am indebted to Him forever for what He has done for me.

The majority of people come into this world with a parent or parents who have hopes and aspirations that their children will be someone successful. Parents sacrifice a great deal of time and resources to give their children the opportunity to succeed. Jesus was sent into this world by His Father to die for sinners. If you are a parent, I have to ask you this question: Would you give your beautiful child to suffer a bloody, brutal death on a cross for someone who deserved to die? Stop and meditate on that awesome thought for a moment. Jesus' sole purpose for coming into this world was to destroy the works of the devil by laying down His life for you and for me. You can't find a greater love than the love our Heavenly Father has for us. Agape love is the highest form of love because it is given with no motivation of self gain. The sole purpose of this kind of love is so the recipient can receive the blessing from a selfless form of love. I did not know that love when I ran the streets selling drugs, drinking, and filling my soul with fornication and adultery. I might not have known it if not for the prison sentence, and that is why I sincerely believe that we have to be taken to a tough place at times so we can begin to look beyond ourselves and realize that we are not the center of the universe. The world does not revolve around us. When I had the money and the honeys, I didn't spend much of my time thinking about God; on the contrary, my time was spent thinking of ways to get more money and more honeys. The only time God came into the equation was when I was in a bad situation that I knew I could not get myself out of. As soon as the situation abated, I went right back to my sinful ways.

The soul is the seat of the human intellect, will, and emotion. When Jesus Christ is not on the throne of the heart of a man, that man's soul is a slave to sin. I believe every human being is birthed into this world with a void in their soul, which can only be filled or satisfied with the love of Jesus. I know we like to look at the cute, cuddly baby as an innocent little child, but trust me when I tell you that the little bundle of joy was born with a propensity and a proclivity to do bad things. Why do you think he has to be taught how to do right, and has a tendency to deviate to mischievous behavior? Once his nature begins to interact with people, places, and things in his environment, he will exhibit behavior patterns that have to be corrected. Some individuals will be more devious than others in their choices and their behaviors, but it is not a matter of *if* there will be deviant, sinful behavior but of *how much.*

I believe the use of illicit drugs, the desire for illicit sex, and the desire for material things are an indication that the soul of the individual is yearning and longing for something that is missing. The missing link is the restoration of the relationship our forefather Adam had with his God Yahweh when he walked and talked with Him in the cool of the day. I know it is difficult for non-Christians to comprehend a God who walks and talks with his children, but He loves us and that is why He condescends to be with us. When I received the revelation of what Jesus had done for me on March 6, 1991, I knew I had to serve Him. I knew I wanted to spend the rest of my life doing the work of the Evangelist. You must understand, "to whom much is given much is required." This is a true statement, and since Jesus gave His life for me, my life now belongs to Him. Exchange is no robbery, so I willingly submit and yield to His authority. Do I rebel sometimes? Of course I do. The old sin nature didn't die when Jesus saved me; it just went undercover because my spirit man was made alive. The sin nature is always looking for a way to bounce back, so I realized I had to stay focused during my tenure in prison because it was easy to slip into perdition. The English prison was full of cheap, homemade liquor called, "hooch," and the inmates smuggled in weed, hashish, heroin, and other contraband. The majority of inmates continue to get their hustle on when they are locked up. The game does not stop because someone is in prison. They hustle cigarettes and sell the drugs they are able to smuggle in on their visits. In the English prison, an inmate can fornicate and commit adultery because we were allowed to have private visits with females—arranged by the vicar of the Church of England of all people.

When Jesus Christ comes on board and sits on an individual's heart, that individual has a desire to live a better life. He or she still has to fight the good fight of faith, but now with Jesus they can win the cosmic struggle between flesh and spirit. I wish every prisoner and every person in general could experience the life-transforming power of Jesus, as I did. For me, Jesus is the only answer to a sin sick soul because it is only through His blood that we can receive the pardon we need from God. The demarcation line between Jesus Christ and the gods of the religions of the world is the blood. The religions of the world can tell you how to pray and do good deeds in hopes of attaining a right standing with their god, but they can't offer the one thing needed to achieve that standing—that one thing is the Blood of Jesus Christ, the Lamb of God.

When I found out about the power in His blood, I was overjoyed because my sins were like scarlet. I like to say that Shout could not take the stain out, and Calgon could not take it away. Shout and Calgon were two detergents that were popular when I was younger. You don't hear a lot about the Blood of Jesus much, but without it there can be no remission of sins, and certainly no cleansing from the stain of sin. Prior to giving my heart to the Lord in prison, my life was filthy, and I felt powerless when I tried to stop some of the things in which I engaged in. As a matter of fact, there were some things I did not want to stop because my flesh enjoyed them, even though they were not good for me. People don't sin because it makes them feel bad; they do it because it satisfies something within them. It is akin to taking a poison that tastes good but is killing you, softly and slowly.

We need to be honest and admit that sin is pleasurable to the carnal man, but if not dealt with, it will eventually lead to death and destruction. It's a shame that it took time in prison for me to learn this valuable lesson, but given the choice of learning that lesson in prison or living life on the outside without it, I would choose the prison sentence every time; with that knowledge I was set free, although I was in prison. I didn't take the time to study the Bible before I went to prison because it was all about the life of pleasure. The Word of God is of the utmost importance because it is the light that can shine in the darkest recesses of our souls. It is the thing that gives us the road map to eternal life and the instructions on how to avoid the pitfalls that litter the landscape of our lives. The problem is, although the Bible is all around us, many people don't think they need to read it and live by the writing on its pages. Most Christians probably don't read the Bible as often as they should. Let me make it a bit more personal. I know I don't read it as much as I should, so I know that an individual outside of life in Jesus Christ is reading very little of it, if any at all. The Apostle Paul summed it up best when he wrote, *"But if our gospel be hid, it is hid to them that are lost: in whom the god of this world has blinded the minds of them which believe not, lest the light of the glorious gospel of Christ, who is the image of God, should shine unto them" (2 Corinthians 4:4).*

The great deception has to be in the fact that the majority of people who are blind don't know they are blind. We must never forget that Satan is a master illusionist who deceives people into thinking wrong is right and right is wrong. We must also remember that he will make dark things seem like light in order to entice us. Godly discernment is absolutely necessary if we are to avoid this deception. Please do not think that is impossible for the devil to deceive you and me, because the Bible declares, *"And no marvel; for Satan himself is transformed into an angel of light. Therefore it is no great thing if his ministers also be transformed as the ministers of righteousness; whose end shall be according to their works" (2 Corinthians 4:14).* Greater individuals than you and I have been deceived by the devil, so don't think for a moment because you are a Christian you can underestimate him. Jesus said he had to shorten the days so the elect would not be deceived. Now that I am in Christ, I can see the level of deception upon which I operated in the world. I used to read Psalms because I thought I could receive protection from God, but I refused to surrender to the Lord of the Psalms. I used to ask God to help me when I was in trouble, but I had no intention of serving Him once the trouble was gone. I was blinded by the god of this age, but when Jesus turned the lights on, I made a commitment to walk in the light and to help others to do so. I didn't have a church or a pulpit, but I had a captive audience with a great deal of time on their hands.

Most inmates are very well read because they have so much time to read and to study. They are also some of the healthiest individuals because of their strict discipline in keeping their bodies in shape. I know I spent countless hours working out in my cell and trying to eat as healthy as possible—although the latter can be very challenging in a prison environment.

One of the exciting things about a new convert to Christ is the zeal for witnessing. Most Christians will tell you how eagerly they shared their faith as a newborn babe in Christ. For some reason, as people grow older in Christ, they witness less. I guess it is because by that time, most of their social interaction is with other believers in Christ, whereas, the babes in Christ are not far removed from their old friends. Soul winning through evangelism should be the heartbeat of every Christian because it is the heartbeat of Jesus. There is an old adage that states, "Birds of a feather flock together." It is difficult to witness to sinners if we are not willing to go out of our way to engage them. Most of us do not work well with rejection, so we are timid about approaching strangers to tell them that Jesus saves and satisfies. The new babe in Christ is not worried too much about getting rejected because fresh in his mind are all the sins from which the Lord has delivered him.

Living a life for Jesus in prison is not easy because you have to have a certain amount of machismo about you since you are constantly being tested. Can you imagine turning the other cheek in prison? I wrestled with that verse for some time because I knew the time would come when I would have to defend myself. When the time came, Jesus worked out the situation wonderfully. I was in the gym working out, and some nut case got into an argument with me, picked up a weight, and threatened me with it. I just stood firm and stared straight into his eyes, trying my best to show no fear. The eyes are the mirror to the soul, and you can look in the eyes of an individual and discern whether they are going to fight or flee. The crazed inmate with the weight stood in front of me ranting about bashing my head in, but I just kept looking into his eyes. He seemed to be frozen in his tracks. Eventually the guards came over and took him away. The Christian in prison is like a lamb among wolves, so he has to be as gentle as a dove but as wise as a serpent. I do not believe that Jesus is instructing us to allow people to walk over us when He tells us to turn the other cheek. We have to seek peace with all men, but we have to defend ourselves if put to the test. The Lord gave me boldness for witnessing to other inmates, and I was willing to come beyond my fears and my comfort level to be that witness for Him. My love and appreciation for Him overrode any fear or trepidation

I had about witnessing. The Holy Ghost on the inside of me gave me the boldness to spread the gospel in the prison. *"Not by might, nor by power, but by the spirit, saith the LORD of hosts" (Zechariah 4:6).*

Jehovah-sabaoth—The Lord of Hosts

The LORD of Hosts is Jehovah-sabaoth, and He fights our battles and delivers us from our enemies. He is able to pull us out of the pit and the miry clay. When we are overwhelmed and at the point of defeat, when we are surrounded by enemies, when there appears to be darkness all around, there is a name that we can call on, and He will fight the battle for us. On page 103 of her book, *The Peace & Power of Knowing God's Name,* author Kay Arthur declared, *"When there seemed to be no other recourse for deliverance, the children of Israel came to know God as Jehovah-sabaoth. It is God's name for man's extremity. And it is not until we, as God's redeemed people, find ourselves failing and powerless that we realize our need to run into the strong tower of His name."*

"The name of the Lord is a strong tower: the righteous runneth into it, and is safe" (Proverbs 18:10). The Lord's name is a tower of strength that is impregnable and impenetrable. His name cannot be pierced or penetrated by the fiery darts of the wicked one. He has given us the power and the authority to use His name. I am overjoyed at the fact that He does not pull us out of the pit to leave us in a proverbial "no man's land." He pulls us out of the pit for a purpose, and that purpose is for us to dwell in His presence. The psalmist declared, *"Thou wilt shew me the path of life: in thy presence is fullness of joy; at thy right hand there are pleasures for evermore" (Psalm 16:11).*

His right Hand is a symbol of strength, power, and action. It is indicative of His Divine protection. I experience the Divine protection of the Hands of the Lord of Hosts many times in my life, and I thank Him for fighting the battles for me. In this season of turmoil and uncertainty, this season when things are being shaken, this season where the devil and his minions are attacking from every side, rest in the name of Jehovah-sabaoth—the Lord of hosts. The psalmist declared, *"He that dwelleth in the secret place of the most High shall abide under the shadow of the Almighty. I will say of the Lord, He is my refuge and my fortress: my God; in him will I trust" (Psalm 91:1-2).*

We must trust Him to protect us from hurt, harm, and danger. We cannot win the battles on our own, but with him we are certain of victory. Hallelujah!!!

CHAPTER 8

From the Pig Pen to the Palace

<u>The Pig Pen</u>

After receiving the eight-year sentence, I was sent to a prison on the Isle of Sheppy, a place called Swaleside. An eight-year sentence is a pretty long stretch, but I was encouraged by the fact that I did not have a life sentence and time does not stand still. I decided to take it one day at a time knowing that one day, the sentence would be over. Serving a prison sentence is more mental than physical because the claustrophobic conditions and the violent nature of the environment wears down the mind as time progresses. If you can avoid being stabbed, then you will be all right physically—because there is a lot of time to exercise. Many prisoners look like Hercules in their body, but mentally you can tell they do not have it all together.

I was determined not to fall into a pit of depression and melancholy. I could not help the fact that I was in a physical pit, but I could control my state of mind. I knew I was there because of decisions that I'd made, so I knew I had to man up and be ready to do all eight years if necessary.

In the Bible, the number eight is symbolic of new beginnings. I arrived at Swaleside prison as a new creature in Christ, with a life that was washed in the blood of the Lamb. I came to prison as a reckless individual who cared only about pleasing himself, but I was transformed through the resurrection power of the Lord Jesus, so it was truly a new beginning for me. I had a great deal of peace because I knew God was in control of my life and all things would be well. Prior to my incarceration, I made decisions that could have ruined my life had Jesus not intervened. Whatever I had to face in Swaleside, I would be able to face it because Jesus was on board, and He said He would never leave me nor forsake me. When Jesus is with us, and we yield to His Lordship, He helps us to overcome difficult circumstances. We will have a difficult time dealing with the hard times in our lives if we try to handle things with our own strength. Jesus said, *"Take my yoke upon you, and learn of me; for I am meek and lowly in heart: and ye shall find rest unto your souls. For my yoke is easy, and my burden is light" (Mark 11:29-30).* Arrogance, pride, and a sense of invincibility led me to the pit of prison. Before prison, I was physically free but imprisoned to the lifestyle created from dealing drugs. My body was free, but I had no peace of mind.

There was a time on the streets when I ran into a girl with whom I had gone to high school. She told me that she had seen me on the streets one day and approached me to say hello but was scared off by the look in my eyes. I am not surprised by the fact that I had a crazed looked in my eyes because life in the streets kept me on edge. It felt like there were walls closing in on me. I partied heavily and drank a lot, so my eyes were blood shot red, and I was on edge because of the lack of sleep.

When Jesus came into my heart, I received rest for my soul and learned to humble myself. The life of a drug dealer is very hedonistic and self-centered. When you have access to a lot of money and a lot of women, there is a tendency to think more highly of yourself than you should. My prison sentence was very sobering and made me realize that it was not all about me.

My goal was to study the Word of God so I could learn as much as I could about the Father, Jesus, and the Holy Ghost. I was a new creature in Christ, and if I wanted to grow then I would have to grow from reading and studying His Word daily. It boggles my mind when I see Christians that are nonchalant about God's word. My passion for His word stems from the fact that my life was radically changed for the better through the reading of the Word of God. My radical transformation in prison convinced me that the Bible is the living Word of God and has the key to eternal life. In many countries, people have to hide and read their Bibles. I heard that in the underground church in China, the believers have to memorize large portions of the Bible because of the shortage of Bibles, and because of the crackdown on those churches by the communist government. In the United States, we have the Word of God at our disposal, but many people do not take advantage of its availability by having consistent Bible study.

If you are reading this from a prison cell, I want to encourage you to rest in the Lord and learn all you can about Him by studying His word. His word will reveal mysteries to you that will strengthen your walk with Him. Commit the scriptures to memory and live by the teachings of Jesus. Allow His Word to cleanse you. I know that the prison environment is a vicious one, but God has you in the place of purpose because He did not allow you to die in your sins. Allow Him to free your mind and use you to be an instrument and a witness for His Glory. I was in the same place you are now, so I know how the prison environment can wear down your mind. You must remember that He will keep in perfect peace those whose minds are focused on Him. I faced some tough situations when I was locked up, but He brought me through them all.

The mind has to be kept active in a prison environment. I believe every inmate should spend as much time as possible reading so their minds can be strengthened. If you did not get a high school diploma or a college degree on the outside, then use your time of incarceration to pursue your high school equivalency diploma and your college degree. You cannot do anything about the decisions that led you to prison, but you can use your time there to better yourself. Free your mind from perverse thoughts, and you will not act in ways that are self-destructive and detrimental to society.

I understood that it did not make sense to spend hours working out in the gym and in my cell to have a muscular looking body only to spend very little time exercising my mind through study. It is good to have balance in one's life. I wanted to learn Spanish, so I got my hands on some books and tapes and began to practice. I enrolled in a computer class while I was on remand and learned to type. I am glad I did because learning to type has helped me immensely in typing the manuscript for my books. Man can cage our bodies, but we must not allow our thoughts to be caged. In prison, it is very easy to settle into the grind of prison life. I decided that I was going to do the time, and the time was not going to do me. I was not going to allow my mind to suffer erosion through a lack of mental stimulation. I was not going to pervert my thoughts with pornographic or secular magazines and books that feed a carnal mind. I purposed in my heart to leave prison a better person than when I entered, and I knew that would be made possible by meditating on the Word of God. I wanted to be like David, the man after God's own heart, who hid God's word in his heart so he would not sin against Him. I took the first step towards achieving that goal of leaving prison a changed person for the better when I asked the Lord Jesus to come into my heart and be the Lord of my life. As far as God was concerned, I was a new babe before Him. My slate was wiped clean, and it was up to me to make sure that good things were written on it going forward.

The death, burial, and the resurrection power of Jesus had set me free, and I was determined not to be like the individuals described in *2 Peter 22* as *"the dog that is turned to his own vomit again; and the sow that was washed to her wallowing in the mire."* Old habits die hard, and the prison environment was a place where it was easy to fall back into sinful habits. Once I knew that I would not be going home for several years, I came up with a mental strategy on how I would make my time as productive as possible. I knew that I had to find people in the prison who were saved. I had no intention of hanging out with the kinds of characters with whom I hung out on the streets. Association brings on assimilation, so I knew I had to associate myself with other inmates who were saved and serious about the things of God.

One of the things I noticed about the English prison system that was different from the American prison system was that I did not experience the horror and the violence about which I'd read and heard in the prisons in the United States. Please do not get me wrong. I am not saying there is no violence in English prisons, because I witnessed it first hand. I am saying that from my experience, there was not as much violence in the places I spent my time. Swaleside was a category B prison. It was a training prison, so I took advantage of the computer classes they offered and learned to type. I did not know that the typing lessons would help me in the future with the manuscripts I had to write. Time is precious, and the inmate with a lot of time on his hands should use that time wisely by partaking in activities that elevate the mind. Although Swaleside was a category B, there were some "dog heart" individuals there. "Dog heart" is a term used in Jamaica for a cold-hearted killer.

In American prisons, there are a great deal of stabbings, robberies, and even rape. If you show weakness in the American prison system, your manhood will be taken and you will become someone's girl. It is a vicious environment that has destroyed the lives of many inmates. I am sure a lot of the American prisoners have to join gangs just to protect themselves. When I was in England, I did not hear of any inmates being raped. It probably happened in some places, but thank God I was spared from a lot of the seedy things that happen in prison. It is bad enough to lose your freedom, but a person should not have to worry about someone stabbing them in their back or getting gang raped by a bunch of macho individuals who cannot control their desire to dominate other men. When you see some of the ingenuous things some inmates do to create weapons, you have to marvel. It would be an awesome thing if the inmates used their time and energy to study and learn a trade that will help them to better themselves and society. I guess, for most people to survive in a violent prison environment, they have to act like the people around them. Once again, association leads to assimilation. I guess in their minds, they figure if the other guy is armed then they have to be armed, too.

Once I put my life in the Hands of God, and trusted Him to protect me, I had peace. I was not going to join the Nation of Islam or any other group to get protection in prison. As far as I was concerned, I had angels assigned to me by my Heavenly Father and nothing could penetrate their defense. I refused to walk around paranoid that some nut would sneak up on me and stab me or bust me upside the head. I did not drink anymore; I did not gamble or use drugs, so I avoided a great deal of confrontations by my abstinence from those activities. My one desire and goal was to know the Lord that saved me and to know Him in an intimate way.

Prior to being locked up in prison, I spent many years feeding the flesh with alcohol, illicit sex, and many other vices. As far as I was concerned, I had a lot of time to make up. I was reading my little New

Testament voraciously before I received the eight-year sentence, and I made up my mind to take my reading and studying to another level. I had no doubt that the key to my Christian development rested in knowing as much as I could about Jesus, then living according to the instructions found in the Bible. I did not have that desire when I was free because I was under the total domination of my carnal nature. I was a slave to sin and was only interested in the things that made my flesh feel good. I was made alive in Christ on that evening of March 6, 1991, and I wanted to do everything I could to continue to live for the Lord Jesus. The devil had me bound when I ran the streets, and he would have killed me if Jesus had not saved me and set me on course for the abundant life.

Rev. John Wilbur Chapman wrote these words in the hymn "Oh Glorious Day": *"Living He loved me, dying He saved me, Buried He carried my sins far away. Rising He justified freely forever, One day He's Coming-Oh Glorious Day!"*

My life in prison was a disciplined life because I knew I had wasted valuable time on the outside. I had been reckless with my freedom, and when you are reckless with your freedom, you will lose it. I decided to be diligent with the time I had going forward. When my children were growing up, I told them that with freedom comes responsibility, and when you are irresponsible with your freedom, you will lose it. I told them that priority meant putting the most important things first. One of the great tragedies of life is living in mediocrity and never fulfilling one's God-given potential. There are many people in prisons all over the world who have the IQ to become a CEO, a doctor, a lawyer, or some other professional, but a lack of discipline, a propensity, a larcenous proclivity, and a desire to take the easy way out caused them to underachieve. There are many inmates who know the law because they spend many hours in law libraries searching for information that will help a fellow inmate with their appeal. Because your body is incarcerated, it does not mean that your mind has to be.

I was determined not to wake up one day having regrets because I never fulfilled my potential. My yesterdays were gone into eternity, and the tomorrows were not promised, so I decided to take advantage of the gift that was the present day. When you waste a great deal of time in the streets committing crimes, it is time you will not get back. Once my eyes were opened to the fact that I had not accomplished much during my days in the streets, I arose with a sense of urgency. It is that urgency that drives me today to be all I can be in God. I could not undo the fact that I was a felon, but that would not be the ending to my life story. Many people cannot understand why I am so driven when it comes to the things of God, but my gratitude for what Jesus did for me compels me to press on for the mark of the prize of the high calling in Christ Jesus. The Apostle told the Corinthians, *"For the love of Christ constraineth us; because we thus judge, that if one died for all, then were all dead: And that he died for all, that they which live should not henceforth live unto themselves, but unto him which died for them, and rose again"* (2 Corinthians 5:14-15).

The Greek word for constraineth is *sunecho* (pronounced *soon-ekh-o*) and it means *to compel*, to *hold*, or to *keep in*. It also means *to arrest*. When you are arrested by the love of Jesus Christ and recognize the richness of His love, you have a great desire to give Him your all. Agape love is the kind of love that caused Jesus to be spat upon, beaten to a bloody pulp, and nailed to a cross for a debauched sinner. This is an unsearchable kind of love. When you experience that kind of love, you will never be the same again.

Many people talk about jailhouse religion in a condescending way, but I did not find religion, I found a Savior, and his name is Jesus Christ. He does not offer religion but a relationship and a covenant that is unsurpassed. I am one individual who does not believe in biting the hands that feed him. Once I realized that Jesus made the ultimate sacrifice for me by dying on the cross, I knew that I was going to be steadfast in following Him. I knew the prison environment would not be the easiest place to walk and live as a Christian, but Jesus gave His all for me, and I was determined to give my all to Him. I was very zealous and bold for the things of God and was hungry for more. When I was in the world, I did not realize that I was under the control of the devil because of my life of rebellion. Jesus spoke about the spirit of rebellion that works in the children of disobedience. The devil was the first one to rebel when He decided to try and exalt himself above the Almighty God. When he failed, he caused Adam to rebel by deceiving Eve. When Adam disobeyed God, every man after Adam born with the Adamic nature has an innate desire to be independent of God. I was no different, and my actions proved it. I just didn't have the full understanding of the fact that the devil was behind it. I thought I was just doing my own thing.

Men will create gods for themselves that allow them to live a pseudo spiritual lifestyle and not feel conviction. Yahweh is a Holy God, and we have to sanctify ourselves in order to enter into His presence. When He was ready to speak to the Israelites, the Bible declares, *"And the LORD said unto Moses, Go unto the people, and sanctify them to day and tomorrow, and let them wash their clothes, And be ready against the third day: for the third day the LORD will come down in the sight of all the people upon mount Sinai" (Exodus 19:10-11).* The third day is akin to the seventh day in that it is symbolic of Divine perfection and completion. Jesus took three disciples with Him on the mount of transfiguration, and they saw three glorified bodies—Jesus, Moses, and Elijah. Hosea 6:2 declares, *"After two days will he revive us: in the third day he will raise us up, and we shall live in his sight."* Jesus Christ rose from the grave on the third day with all power. The Lord is pulling people out of the pit of sin in order to sanctify them for the third-day visitation. When I was in the streets drinking, fornicating, and committing adultery, I had no clue or concept of this. My conscience told me that my lifestyle was wrong, but I seared my conscience so I could partake in the sins of the carnal nature.

I did not know that I was just a puppet on a string being dangled around by the devil. Make no mistake; no one is totally independent in this life. If an individual's life is not in Jesus Christ, then he or she is being controlled by the devil. I know some people believe the devil is a figment of an overactive imagination, and Christianity is a crutch, but that is exactly how the devil deceives people. I was totally deceived, like many other people, but now my eyes were opened. As hard as I'd worked to satisfy my fleshly urges, I decided I would work even harder to feed my spirit man. The thing you feed is the thing that will gain strength. If you feed the carnal man, then he will grow strong and dominate your life. If you feed your spirit man, then you will have dominion over your carnal nature. It is not easy to keep the spirit strengthened because daily we are bombarded with images that stimulate our carnal nature. This is why the Bible instructs us to "die daily." We can strengthen the spirit man through study and meditation of the Word of God, through fasting and prayer, and through praise and worship. The flesh is like a weed that, if left unchecked, will take over the whole garden. Notice how much work you have to put into creating a beautiful garden. Weeds seem to grow on their own, but flowers have to be cared for continually. Jesus created the garden when He died on the cross for our sin, and the Father sent the Holy Ghost to be the gardener who keeps the garden looking beautiful. He will weed and feed our lives to keep us looking beautiful in the realm of the spirit, but we have to yield to the process in order to avoid our lives being overrun by the weeds created by the flesh.

I tell people all the time that the trials they experience in their Christian walk is like the dung that is used to fertilize plants. We love to eat the fruit, but who wants to till the soil and lay down the fertilizer? It takes work to maintain a beautiful garden, and that is why some people have beautiful gardens and some have gardens that are overgrown with weeds. Solomon declared, *"I went by the field of the slothful, and by the vineyard of the man void of understanding; And, lo, it was all grown over with thorns, and nettles had covered the face thereof, and the stone wall was broken down. Then I saw, and considered it well: I looked upon it, and received instruction. Yet a little sleep, a little, slumber, a little folding of the hands to sleep: So shall thy poverty come as one that travelleth; and thy want as an armed man"* (Proverbs 24:30-34). An individual will be void of understanding when he is unwilling to submit to the Lord. Psalm 119:125-126 declares, *"I am thy servant; give me understanding, that I may know thy testimonies. It is time for thee, LORD, to work: for they have made void thy law. Verse 130 declares, "The entrance of thy words giveth light; it giveth understanding unto the simple."*

We cannot afford to be slothful and lazy when it is time to read, study, and to meditate on God's word. We have to exercise wisdom; we have to be on guard constantly because the enemy wants to lull us to sleep so he can sow tares in our fields. The stone wall was broken down, and that meant there was no protection. The Bible declares, *"He that diggeth a pit shall fall into it; and whoso breaketh an hedge, a serpent shall bite him"* (Ecclesiastes 10:8). The only way the serpent was able to bite Job was when God took down the hedge. He was able to bite Adam and Eve because Adam's sin of rebellion caused the hedge to come down. We have to be proactive, and we have to be on guard against the wiles and the trickery of the serpent the devil. When we become slothful and derelict in our spiritual duties, our spiritual hedge will come down, and that serpent the devil will bite us. With this in mind, I knew that I had to walk circumspect in the things of the Lord in prison. There were vipers all around me, and I had to use godly discernment and wisdom, but most of all I had to be proactive in prayer, studying God's Word and worship.

The Prodigal

When I entered the floor on the Isle of Sheppy where my cell was located and looked at the names and sentences of the other inmates, I gasped for air and realized I was in the big leagues. Next to the majority of names was the word "Life." I realized right away that the majority of the inmates on the floor were in prison for murder. All of a sudden, the eight years did not seem that much after all. My sentence was the lowest of all the sentences on that floor. I found out later that some of the men had already been in prison for over a decade. Barring an unforeseen circumstance, my mandatory time to be served before I could be released was five years and four months. I wanted to keep my nose clean so I could return to my wife and children as soon as possible, but I realized that it would take a great deal of discipline to stay above the fray. I would learn that discipline once I set my mind to be a disciple of Christ. It is not a coincidence that disciple and discipline have the same root. There is no place in the scripture where Jesus said we should make members. He said, "Go into all the world and make disciples." Unfortunately, many Christians are so bogged down with the cares of this life that they do not have the discipline, the time, or the commitment level required to be a disciple. An excellent example of the difference between the disciple and the member can be found in a story in the Bible about one of Jesus' visits to the home of Martha and her sister Mary.

Are You Troubled about Many Things?

Martha extended an invitation to Jesus to visit her home. The Bible described Martha's sister, Mary, as one who sat at Jesus' feet and heard His word. Feet are symbolic with our walk with the Lord, and faith comes by hearing His word. It is impossible to please him without faith, and that is why we need to find time to sit at His Feet and glean from His words. Disciples willingly make the necessary sacrifices and spend many hours at the feet of Jesus gleaning from His words. In stark contrast to Mary, Martha was cumbered about much serving. The word cumbered in Greek is, *perispao* (pronounced *per-ee-spah-o)*, and it means *to drag all around, to distract with care.* Stop dragging the cares of this world and the hurts from the past around like a ball and chain. Jesus has set you free, so do not be entangled with the yoke of bondage.

When Jesus is in the house, all extracurricular activities and chores must cease because the place to be at that point is at His Feet worshiping Him and receiving His word. Martha actually tried to get Jesus to send Mary to help her with the serving. There is nothing wrong with serving, but there is a time and a place for everything. I love Jesus' response to Martha. He said, *"Martha, Martha, thou art careful and troubled about many things: but one thing is needful: and Mary hath chosen that good part, which shall not be taken away from her" (Luke 10: 40-41).* It appears there were some underlying things going on in the life of Martha that went beyond the serving because the Lord said, *"she was troubled about many things."* My question is, how can someone be troubled when the Lord Jesus is in the house? All cares must be cast upon Him because His yoke is easy and His burden is light.

The one thing that was needful was to be at the feet of Jesus, and Mary had chosen it. We all have the same amount of hours in the day, and we choose how we allocate those hours. Mary chose to sit at the feet of the Master while Martha chose to busy and trouble herself with a lot of serving. There are many people who love the Lord but are constantly distracted by the issues of everyday life. We need to understand that a lot of the things we do will be burned up in the fire, and we will not receive credit for them, so we'd better learn to prioritize. The good part will never be taken away from the disciple because the good part will carry them throughout eternity.

Prison is full of unforeseen circumstances because of the violent nature of the prisoners. I realized that most of these inmates on the floor weren't getting out for a long time and might frown upon a short timer like myself. I knew I had to tread lightly, but I also knew that I had to stand like a man. I made a choice that come what may, my stance would be that of a Man of God. Like Martha's house, Jesus was residing in my house, and I was going to make sure that He had my full attention and total control of my house. It was not a cake walk because there were many distractions, snares, and pitfalls, but my eyes were on the prize. As foresaid, it was not going to be easy, but if discipleship was easy, then all believers would be disciples. Prison is not the place you want to be, but the plus side, if there was one, was that I had a great deal of time to dedicate to learning the things of God by studying His word.

On the Isle of Sheppy, I disciplined myself with bodily exercise and much study of the word. One of the amazing things about the Word of God is, the more you study it, the more you want to study it. The more of the Word I learned, the more I wanted to learn because learning taught me how much I did not know, and how deceived I was when I did not submit my life to the Lordship of Jesus Christ. Many people think they know God, but the main way He reveals Himself is through His word; that is why the Bible declares, *"The Word became flesh and dwelt among us."* He did it so we could learn about the Father. Jesus is the perfect image of the Father, and it is impossible to learn about God the Father without knowing Jesus. *"For in him dwelleth the fullness of the Godhead bodily" (Colossians 2:9).*

Time spent on the Isle of Sheppy was not like time spent on a Caribbean vacation. In the summer time, I found out that the prison was located next to a pig farm. When the wind blew, the stench from the pigs would permeate my cell and practically suffocate me. I had fallen very far from the days of relaxing on the pristine beaches of my beautiful homeland of Jamaica. On many occasions, I thought about the phrase I quoted earlier: **Sin will take you farther than you want to go; keep you longer than you want to stay; and cost you more than you want to pay.** Every part of that adage was true for me because I was far away from home; I was locked in a place where I had no desire to stay; and I was paying a high price, which was my freedom.

114

Accommodations were meager in that I had to sleep in a cell in a bed with blankets that had been used by previous inmates. The cuisine certainly was not from any five-star restaurants. If you think hospital food is bad, you should try eating some of the slop served in prison. I ate a lot of oatmeal because I found it more palatable. I did not eat oatmeal much when I was free because I had a lot of choices in terms of what I could eat, but in prison I did not have that luxury. I learned to love the oatmeal because it was nutritious. You can imagine how devastated I was when a fellow inmate told me that on the bags of oatmeal that I loved so much was a stamp that read, "Pigs meal." The inmates had to eat the same oatmeal that was used to fatten the pigs.

In the natural, I had fallen so far that I was eating the same meal pigs ate. I was indeed like the prodigal in terms of my cuisine, but in the realm of the spirit, I was soaring. Jesus had given me a new lease on life, and I was not about to allow the environs of the pig pen to depress my mind. A relationship with Jesus can help you to transcend the boundaries of a depressing state or environment. I was so wrapped up in learning about Jesus that I had no time to be depressed about where I was. I missed my wife and children terribly, but I knew that in Christ, I was going to return home a new and improved husband and father. It was only a matter of time, so I made sure that that time was spent wisely.

My experience on the Isle of Sheppy left an indelible impression on my psyche. I was stripped of my fancy clothes, I had no champagne to drink, and there were no women, just a bunch of males—and those males were not choirboys. I was reduced to being a number and had to march to the beat of the prison guards. They told me when I could get out of my cell to eat, and when to turn in for the night. Life on the Isle of Sheppy taught me that a man without Jesus is like a pig wallowing in a sty.

The story of the prodigal son found in the book of Luke is special to me because it contains many parallels to my own life. One of the best examples of the manner in which God will take a sinner out of the pit of sin and the pig sty, clean him up, and take him to the palace or the kingdom is found in this story in Luke 15:11–32. I read the story countless times when I was at Swaleside, and every time I read it the Lord gave me new revelation. It is a great lesson for everyone—especially young people who feel they can do better if they are independent of their parents' rules and regulations. Please allow me to dissect this wonderful story for you.

The Bible says the younger of two sons came to his father and requested that his father give him the portion of inheritance that was his. It was an unusual request because the older son was in line to get his inheritance first, and that would happen when the father was about to die. *"A good man leaveth an inheritance to his children's children." (Proverbs 13:22b).* "Younger son" in scripture can speak of a level of immaturity as well as a person's chronological age. The Bible says the father divided his possessions among them. The older son stayed home, but the younger son gathered all his things and traveled to a far country, and there wasted his substance with riotous living.

Allow me to exegete this first portion of the text: The younger son represents the gentiles who are separated from God because of their rebellion. The older son represents a Pharisaical religious people bound by legalism and the traditions of men. It is important to note the fact that the younger son took all his things, showing his desire to sever all ties to his father's house. This point is enforced when we examine his destination and the purpose of his trip. He took his journey into a far country and wasted his substance with riotous living. The result of his trip shows that he was not mature enough to handle the inheritance. Many young people want things now, but they do not understand that they will be tested, tempted, and tried; if they are not mature, they will implode through bad decision making.

The younger son was willing to remove himself from the covering of his father's house in order to indulge in the lust of the flesh. Many young people say they cannot wait until they turn eighteen so they can leave their parents' home. If they knew what awaited them, they would stay home as long as possible. I look at my own life as an example and can honestly say that I am still dealing with the repercussions of youthful decisions made because I desired to be independent before I had the maturity to handle that independence. The irony of the whole thing is that young people want to be independent of their parents, but it is those same parents who have to bail them out when they fall into a ditch or a pig pen.

After he spent everything, a mighty famine arose in the land, and he had nothing left for sustenance. It is one thing to have no sustenance when the economy around you is good, but it is a totally different thing when you run out of substance and there is a famine around you. The younger son was in a bad state because the Bible describes the famine as a mighty famine. He tried to alleviate his suffering by getting a job with a citizen of the country in which he lived. His boss sent him into his fields to feed swine. Parents want the best for their children, but this employer had no qualms about using him to feed the pigs. There is something very important to glean here. Jesus was speaking primarily to the Pharisees at that time. They were strict Adherents to the Law of Moses, so swine was untouchable. He did not have the desire to stay at his fathers' house where he would be respected and treated as a son, but now he is forced to work for a stranger in his fields feeding swine. Luke's description gives us a vivid picture of how far the younger son had fallen. He became so hungry that he desired to fill his belly with the husk that the swine ate, and no one would give him a meal. When he had substance, he probably had a lot of hangers-on, but now that the substance is gone, he was alone and starving.

When I was running the streets, drinking and partying, I had a lot of so-called friends, but as soon as I got locked up, most of them disappeared. People will hang with you when things are going good, but most of them will not be able to stick with you when you are in a hard place. The prodigal was in a very hard place, and his company was the pigs.

There is a spiritual aspect to this important verse concerning his hunger. His physical hunger was a picture of his spiritual starvation, which was the result of removing himself from his father's house and covering. Verse 17 captures beautifully the due time spoken of by the Apostle Paul in Romans 5:6. It is an awesome revelation of the pivotal moment in time—that *Kairos* moment when an individual has reached the end of his human strength and comes to a realization that he needs the Father. Luke writes, *"And when he came to himself, he said, How many hired servants of my father's have bread enough and to spare, and I perish with hunger! I will arise and go to my father, and will say unto him, father, I have sinned against heaven, and before thee, and am no more worthy to be called thy son: make me as one of thy hired servants"* (Luke 15:17–19). I absolutely love these verses because it provides a beautiful illustration of what we should do when we find ourselves in the pig pen. Don't allow pride and arrogance to keep you stuck with the swine.

The first thing he had to do was come to himself. This simply means that he came to the realization of the wretchedness of his condition. Don't look at your situation through rose colored glasses. Take an honest assessment of your life and be willing to admit that you are not where you should be in God. The second thing he did was to remember that his father's house was a place of provision and abundance. It was such a place of provision that the servants had enough bread and some to spare. You know, the Father's House is an awesome place to be when the servants are living in overflow. Someone really has to be blind not to repent of their sins and accept the salvation God offers through His Son, Jesus. We do not have to live in spiritual and physical poverty; all we need to do is turn and return. Turn from wickedness and turn to the Father. Every individual living outside the ark of safety needs to know that God has everything they stand in need of and more. Jesus is the bread that came down from Heaven to feed all who are hungry for salvation in His name.

I remember a particular passage of scripture that perplexed me when I read it. It is the story of a Canaanite woman who approached Jesus when He came into the coasts of Tyre and Sidon. She cried unto Jesus and asked Him to have mercy on her because her daughter was grievously vexed with a devil. Jesus kept silent, and his disciples asked him to send her away. Jesus told His disciples that He was only sent unto the lost sheep of Israel. The Canaanites were definitely not of the lost sheep of the house of Israel. They were a nation of Baal worshipers. The woman refused to take no for an answer. She came before Jesus worshiping Him and pleaded with Him for help. Jesus said to her, *"It is not meet to take the children's bread and cast it to dogs"* (Matthew 15: 26). When I first read this verse, I was taken aback by the fact that Jesus called the woman a dog. I remember writing to my wife and asking her about that verse. I found out that the term dog was one frequently used by Jews in Jesus' day to describe gentiles. As a matter of fact, the Bible describes those that go back and entangle themselves with the pollutions of the world after they have been delivered as a dog that is turned to his own vomit, and the sow that was washed to her wallowing in the mire *(2 Peter 2:22)*.

We can all learn a lesson on how to persevere until the Lord grants our request from the Canaanite woman. She told Jesus, *"Truth, Lord: Yet the dogs eat of the crumbs which fall from their masters' table" (Matthew 15:27)*. She didn't get an attitude with Jesus; instead, she humbled herself and recognized that what He was speaking was the truth. She knew that although it was the truth, Jesus held the key to her daughter's deliverance, and she would not stop until her daughter received her deliverance. When the Lord points out a truth to us, we must embrace that truth no matter how difficult it is. Truth is not always an easy pill to swallow, but we must swallow it because no matter how bitter it is to our pride, it holds the key to our freedom. Jesus told her she was a woman of great faith and made her daughter whole that same hour.

The point I want you to take away from this story is that you don't have to settle for the crumbs that are falling off someone's table when you are a son or daughter that has access to the whole loaf. If you are in a backslidden condition right now, then take this time to repent and turn back to the Father's House. If you have not confessed Jesus as savior and asked Him to be the Lord of your life, then take this time and do so. Just say, **"Lord Jesus, I am a sinner but I know you shed your blood for my sins. I repent of my sins and I ask you to come into my heart and be the Lord of my life."** If you are a backslider, then repent and return to the Lord. He will receive you.

The prodigal son came to the place of repentance when he realized life outside the father's house was not all that he thought it would be. When we were first introduced to him, he was looking to get as far away from his father's house as he could. After tasting the fruit of riotous living, he is now ready to go back home—not as a son but as a servant. Beloved, you cannot attain to son-ship without a servant's heart. Anytime we allow ourselves to be enticed away from the Father's house because of earthly goods, we can expect to perish both spiritually and physically. The third thing he does after he comes to himself is to arise. Once God opens our eyes and we see that we are in a detestable condition, it's time to arise! Not with an attitude, anger, or with vengeance, but we must arise with a spirit of humility. He decides to go to his father and confess his sin, and inform his father that he is not worthy to be called a son, but a servant. He actually asked the father to make him one of the hired servants. He knew that a servant in the father's house was better off than a son in the world.

When he first went to his father, his request was, "Father, give me." Now that he has been humbled by the pigsty, his new request is, "Father, make me." This should be the cry of every individual. There are many people who are trying to get all they can and can all they get, but material things don't change most people; they only make them more of what they already are. A dope head with a million dollars is exactly that. He is just a dope head with a million dollars. The fact that he gets a million dollars does not sober him up and make him responsible; it gives him a greater opportunity to indulge in more dope.

When the Father makes us, we will be able to handle the things we receive. The young son was motivated by his desire to live independent of his father's house because the grass looked greener on the other side. He did not have the type of discernment that allowed him to see that destruction was ahead of him, and it would be better to stay put until his father decided to give him his inheritance. I tell my own children and other young people who you might be looked at as an adult when you reach a certain age, but you are not truly an independent adult until you can pay bills and be responsible.

I remember when one of my sons came to me and told me, in his own words, that he was grown and wanted to do his own thing. I told him that was okay, but now that he was grown he had to decide which bill he was going to pay, because grown people pay their own bills. You can imagine the look on his face and his response. His response was silence because he had no JOB. Do not get stressed when a young person in your house tells you they are grown, and they want to stay out late; let them know that if they are truly grown, then they need to help with the bills. Make sure your children know that paying a bill does not give them license to sleep out and do anything they desire. Paying bills sets them on the road to being responsible.

Thank God we have a Heavenly Father who loves us enough to work through our issues. The father in the story of the prodigal son never stopped looking for his son's return. He did not hinder him when he wanted his inheritance, but he also did not close his doors to him. There were times when I was so furious with the behavior of some of my children that I told them they could leave the house if they could not follow the rules. Some of them left, and when they did I prayed fervently for the Lord to protect them. I am glad He did because I would not have been able to deal with the guilt if something had happened to them while they were out of the house. God had to remind me that I was young and impetuous once, and felt I needed to be free of my mom's house.

When the young son was a great way off, his father saw him. We are never so far from our Heavenly Father's omnipresent eyes that He is unable to see us. He does not see us superficially, but He is able to peer into the inner chambers of our hearts to discern true desire. Now we see the love and forgiveness of the Father shining like a glorious light. The father had compassion for him, and hugged and kissed him. God is not mad at His sons and daughters who mess up. He is not mad at people trapped in sin. His heart's desire is that they recognize their condition, repent, and head home to the Kingdom as a son or daughter. Religion wants to make us feel like God is angry with us and wants to punish us. God loves you and desires the best for you. If He takes no delight in the death of the wicked, He certainly wants the best for you.

Although the younger son had dishonored the father by taking his inheritance and wasting it, the father did not treat him like a hired servant when he returned. On the contrary. Luke 15:22-23 describes the blessing he receives. *"But the father said to his servants, Bring forth the best robe, and put it on him; and put a ring on his hand, and shoes on his feet: And bring hither the fatted calf, and kill it; and let us eat, and be merry: For this my son was dead, and is alive again; he was lost, and is found. And they began to be merry."* The best robe represents him being back under his chief covering. The ring on his hand represents a signet or a seal of son-ship. The shoes on his feet signified that his walk with his father was back in right standing. The killing of the fatted calf represented his father sacrificing the best for him. The merry celebration is indicative of the celebration that takes place in Heaven when a sinner is converted or a backslider returns.

It is important to note that repentance means more than saying I'm sorry. The Greek word for repentance is *metanoeho*, and it means, *to think differently, to turn*. The younger son had to change the stinking thinking that led him to the pigsty, and so will the individual who does not know Jesus as Lord and Savior. The adversary desires to deceive us into believing we can mess up and undo what God has for us, but this is not so. The Holy Ghost within us will draw us back to the Father no matter how far we have strayed, because greater is He that is in us than he that is in the world. The journey back to the Father is facilitated by the knowledge that He is waiting for His sons and daughters to return so He can get the heavenly party started. The younger son thought he had to go to a far country to get his groove on, but someone once said: *"Ain't no party like a Holy Ghost party, because a Holy Ghost party don't stop."*

With the introduction of the older brother, we see a self-righteous, jealous, and angry person. *"Now his elder son was in the field: and as he came and drew nigh to the house, he heard music and dancing. And he called one of the servants, and asked what these things meant. And he said unto him, Thy brother is come; and thy father hath killed the fatted calf, because he hath received him safe and sound. And he was angry, and would not go in: therefore came his father out, and intreated him. And he answering said to his father, Lo, these many years do I serve thee, neither transgressed I at any time thy commandment: and yet thou never gavest me a kid, that I might make merry with my friends: But as soon as this thy son was come, which hath devoured thy living with harlots, thou hast killed for him the fatted calf"* (Luke 15:25–30).

The older brother had to ask the servants the reason for the celebration. He didn't leave the house, as the younger brother had, but the servants were more privy to the father's business than he was. Many people are in the church, but they are ignorant of the father's business because they lack a servant's heart. His response when his father came out and entreated him is the same response given by people in the bondage of religion when the Holy Spirit visits them to touch their hearts and give them the mind of Jesus. His response was one of anger and a desire to obtain righteousness through works. He was quick to point out that he never transgressed any of the commandments, and his brother had wasted his father's

122

money with harlots. False, hypocritical religion is one of the biggest hindrances to someone receiving salvation. The older son is drawn to the house by the music and dancing; what a powerful indictment against the enemies of worship who level criticism against churches for praising the Lord with music and dancing! The son comes to the house from the field, and instead of going inside and joining the festivities, he asked one of the servants for an explanation. The text says he was angry and would not enter the house when he found out his wayward brother had returned home, and his father had killed the fatted calf.

Many believers are away from the presence of God because of jealousy and anger. His father came out and entreated him to join the festivities. "Entreated" in the Greek language is *Parakaleo*; it means, *to call near, to exhort, to invoke.* It comes from the root "para," which means "beside," and "kaleo," which means, "to call aloud." The father came out to the obstinate son as a comforter because Parakaleo comes from the same root as *parakletos,* which means *a comforter.* Jesus used this word when He told the disciples that the Father would give them another comforter. The father went to his son in the same manner in which the Holy Spirit comes to each person to draw them to Jesus. The older son was more interested in telling the father how much his younger brother had messed up and how he had stayed home and worked hard. God is not interested in our self-righteous works. He is more interested in us showing love, kindness, and mercy to those in bondage seeking a way back home. We have to be willing to embrace the sinner no matter how messed up they are. We don't embrace sin; we show love to the sinner. We must constantly remind ourselves that God had mercy on us when we were the prodigal son or daughter, so we must not be critical of others.

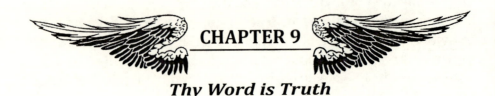

CHAPTER 9

Thy Word is Truth

Taking time to study and meditate on the Word of God during my prison sentence gave me the foundation and the building blocks to grow. I knew the Word of God had the power to transform the heart and mind of the hardest criminal because of the impact it had on me. I did not understand everything in the Word, but I believed by faith that Genesis to Revelation was the God-inspired and the God-breathed truth. I learned early on not to be deceived by a person's religious outlook or religious jargon.

One day, I received a visit from one of the vicars. A vicar is a cleric or a priest who carries out the religious functions in their particular church. I asked him if he believed the story of the flood, and he informed me that there was not an actual flood. I was in shock because I thought as a leader, this man automatically believed that the flood actually happened. One day, I found a book in my cell that spoke about the greatest man who ever lived. I contacted the organization that left the book, and they sent a representative to see me. I noticed that he carried another book besides his Bible, and when I asked him whether we were still supposed to fast, he leafed through the little black book for his answer. He responded by telling me that we don't have to fast anymore, and immediately I remembered that in the Bible we are repeatedly told to fast. My visitor was a Jehovah's Witness, and he was obviously answering me from the doctrine written in the little black book instead of the Bible. I realized that the man to whom they referred as the greatest man who ever lived was not the same man who died on the cross for my sins and set me free. They see Jesus as a great man, but the Bible reveals Him as the Son of God. *"And without controversy great is the mystery of godliness: God was manifest in the flesh, justified in the Spirit, seen of angels, preached unto the Gentiles, believed on in the world, received up onto glory" (1 Timothy 3:16).*

I knew this man was in error, and the book from which he read was also in error. The Apostle Paul told Timothy, *"Now the Spirit speaketh expressly, that in the latter times some shall depart from the faith, giving heed to seducing spirits, and doctrines of devils; speaking lies in hypocrisy, having their conscience seared with a hot iron" (1 Timothy 4:1-2).* Meeting with those two individuals taught me the importance of not being deceived by false teachers.

One evening, I went to mass at the chapel, and the vicar asked me when I was going to be released. I told him that I would be released when God determined that I had learned the lesson that I was there to learn. The man laughed in my face and said, "You mean when your sentence is over." I remember walking back to my cell in total disbelief. I was a young Christian exercising my faith in God, and here was this seasoned Christian looking religious in his collar—but doubting what I believed about my release. Some of the biggest hindrances to people coming into the Kingdom of God are religious people. In one of His many woes to the scribes and Pharisees, Jesus said, *"Woe unto you, scribes and Pharisees, hypocrites! For ye compass sea and land to make one proselyte, and when he is made, ye make him twofold more the child of hell than yourselves" (Matthew 23:15).*

After my experience with the two vicars and the Jehovah's Witness, I made a conscious decision to continue my rigorous diligent study of the Word of God so I would not have to rely on false teachers and doubters who were masquerading in sheep's clothing. I thought about all the individuals who had no clue or concept of the Jesus about which the Bible spoke. I remembered my own state of confusion and wanted to make sure that I did my part to introduce the real Jesus to as many inmates as I could. I started a Bible study in my cell and went witnessing around the prison, inviting other inmates to join me. Soon I had several disciples meeting a couple times a week to study the Word of God. I did not know much, but I was firmly persuaded by what I knew. I knew that the Bible was the Word of God, and it held the key that could unlock the house of bondage, which held the inmates.

I remember one particular inmate who kept coming to the Bible study but would not give up his lifestyle of hustling in the prison. I found out later that he was in prison for a sexual offense, and that meant the rest of the inmates looked at him with disdain. I knew his life would be in danger at some point and thought about distancing myself from him. I never forgot the time the Holy Ghost spoke to my heart and reminded me that I should have died in the streets while I was selling drugs or from AIDS when I lived a life of fornication and adultery. He reminded me that it was because of the mercies of the Lord that I was not consumed, and I should remember those things when I thought about distancing myself from the inmate who was convicted of a sex crime.

I decided to continue to teach him the Word of God, but I warned him to turn from the lifestyle of a hustler and surrender to Jesus. I remember him coming to my cell one day in the summer. I was puzzled by the fact that he had a coat on when the weather was not cold. He appeared to be very nervous and was sweating. I also noticed that he had a broken bottle in his pocket, so I asked him what the problem was. He explained that some inmates were threatening him and a couple of the ones sending the threat were on my floor. A couple of the lifers on my floor found out that he was in for a sex crime, and they were putting the heat on him. There I was harboring him in my cell wondering about my own safety.

Once again, I decided that I was not going to abandon him; I would continue to witness to him. Not long after, someone set a fire in his cell, and the guards were forced to transfer him. I always wondered what became of him. Years later, one of the Bible study disciples phoned me and told me that someone attacked him in another prison and cut his stomach open. I believe he survived the knife attack, but it reminded me of the adage, "crime doesn't pay; it costs."

Delivered from Racial Bitterness

One evening, one of the disciples named Joe asked me if he could bring someone to the Bible study. I said, "Of course." He brought a white guy from Belgium named Paul. Like the rest of us, Paul was in

126

prison for smuggling drugs into England. He was in a very depressed state because his girlfriend had left him and was not allowing him to see his daughter. He had also been attacked and beaten in the previous prison. When Paul joined us, the Lord spoke to my heart and let me know that if I was going to follow Him, I would have to love all people. I had to confront the feelings of bitterness I had because of the attacks I'd suffered over the color of my skin.

Paul accepted Jesus as his personal savior and began to grow in the Lord. As a Christian, he was my brother, and the color of his skin had no bearing on how I interacted with him. Once I got to know him through the fellowship, I realized that he was a good brother and had many personal struggles in his life, just like the rest of us.

Jesus Christ is the only one who can bridge all gaps and things that divide people. He is the only mediator between God and man. He is able to bridge the ethnic, racial, gender, political, financial, and any other divide because He makes us one in Him. In Christ, we are not male or female, black or white, Jew or Gentile, but a new creation. We have to look at each other through the eyes of Jesus and not the eyes of our flesh. Racial, ethnic, and gender segregation is still evident in many churches, but those churches do not paint a true picture of the Church of Jesus Christ. His Church is made up of many tribes and tongues. I am so grateful for what Jesus has done for me that I am willing, with His help, to give up everything that hinders the flow of the Holy Ghost in my life. If you have racism or any other form of intolerance in your heart because of what an individual did to you, then you need to ask the Lord to heal you. Jesus took all our sins when he was on the cross, so we must be willing to forgive others.

We saw great breakthroughs in the lives of the inmates at Swaleside because we prayed, fasted, and witnessed continually. God demonstrated His word in us, and the other prisoners could witness that demonstration. This is the reason why we have to approach the Word of God with a hunger and a thirst. We have to spend time in the Word so He can teach us how to live this Christian life and how to recognize false doctrine. My fellow Bible study students and I took our studies very seriously, and I am glad we did. I had no idea back then that God would use me in the future to travel and do the work of the Evangelist by preaching and teaching His Word. At Swaleside, my study gave me a foundation in the word, and I continue to build on that foundation. I must admit that I don't study as much now as I did then because I don't have as much free time, but I am careful to make sure that I am not neglecting the study of the Word because my lifestyle is too busy.

My pastor, Dr. Samuel N. Greene, constantly reminds us that we cannot be so busy with the work of the Lord that we forget the Lord of the work. We can spend our lives doing a lot of serving, and what an evangelist called "church chores," or we can choose the needful thing. The good part or the needful thing is to sit under the Word of God and receive something that is eternal. The Lord is not saying that we should be derelict in our duties—on the contrary. He wants us to be responsible with the things we have to do, but we must choose to make time for the thing that is most important. We have to learn to prioritize because we live in a very busy society. Everything appears to be moving at a fast pace, and if we are not careful, we can get caught up in the rat race and forget the good part or the needful thing. The temporal things for which we are laboring can be snatched from us at any moment, but the things we receive from the Word of God will carry us throughout eternity.

There are many believers who have labored to own a home; they have put a great deal of time, energy, and resources into their homes only to lose them because of foreclosure. Others have given a great deal of their energies to their employer, and as soon as there is a downturn in the economy, they are given a pink slip or they are downsized because their job is sent overseas. How many others have given themselves in marriage only to see their spouse walk out of the marriage to be with someone else? There is a plethora of other examples I can give, but I know you get the point—and the point is prioritizing the Word of God.

I know beyond a shadow of a doubt that it was the Word of God that strengthened me as a new babe in Christ, and if I expected to stand strong as an adult, then I have to be willing to put in the study time. There were many dark times during my incarceration when I could have fallen into sin and depression, but the Word of God kept me strong and gave me hope. God allowed me to share that same Word with others so they could be strengthened. Let me share a key scripture with you that sums up the importance of the Word of God: *"In the beginning was the word, and the Word was with God, and the Word was God. The same was in the beginning with God. All things were made by him; and without him was not anything made that was made" (John 1: 1-3).* Everything in the universe was created by the Word, so it is important for us to understand that the Word of God has creative ability. If we apply the Word to our lives, we will experience creative miracles. The writer to the Hebrews said God framed the worlds by the Words He spake, so I believe it is possible for us to frame our worlds by speaking His Word. When you face a situation that is adverse, don't allow yourself to speak negative words because life and death are in the power of the tongue. There is a scripture in the Bible for everything you have to deal with, so the more scriptures you have in your heart, the more you will be able to speak and apply to your situation.

I remember reading about Solomon and how the Lord gave him great wisdom because he did not ask for wealth. When I went down on my knees on March 6, 1991 to pray the prayer of repentance, I asked the Lord to give me deep revelation of His Word, and then I asked Him to give me the faith to believe what He revealed to me. When I got up, I got up with a great desire to learn what was in the Word. My motivation was not to become some famous preacher. I wanted to learn so I could live a life that is holy and pleasing to the Lord, but I also wanted to be able to share the Word with people who were struggling. Paul told his son in the faith, Timothy, to, *"study to shew thyself approved unto God, a workman that needeth not be ashamed, rightly dividing the word of truth" (2 Timothy 2:15).* There is a huge difference between reading and studying. Studying takes time, and the aid of Biblical references has to be elicited. Without careful study, we will not be able to rightly divide the Word and be approved or acceptable to God.

The Bible informs us of the benefits we get when we spend time reading and meditating on it. I call Psalm 119 "the word Psalm," because of its many references to the Word of God. Wiersbe's outline of the Old Testament declares this about Psalm 119: "All but five verses mention the Word of God in one way or another. The exceptions are verses 84, 90, 121, 122, and 132. God is referred to in every verse. The number eight is stamped all over this psalm. Each section has eight verses; there are eight special names for God's Word listed; there are eight symbols of the Word given; the believer has eight responsibilities to the Word. The word "eight" in Hebrew literally means *abundance, more than enough*; it is the number of new beginnings. It is as though the writer is saying, "God's Word is enough. If you have the Scriptures, they are all you need for life and godliness." Indeed, the Bible points us to Christ: He is the Living Word about whom the written Word speaks. In one sense, Psalms 119 is an expansion of Psalms 19:7-11. Note the eight basic titles of the Bible in the first nine verses of the psalm: law of the Lord, testimonies, ways, precepts, statutes, commandments, judgments, and word. These are repeated many times throughout the psalm.

The Psalmist said, *"thy word have I hid in mine heart, that I may not sin against thee" (Psalm 119:11).* The word will be hidden in our hearts when we take the time to sit under it and be instructed by someone God has anointed with the gift of teaching.

I have been to many services and listened to the Word of God taught, and I have often wondered whether the speaker spent quality time searching the scriptures before stepping into the pulpit to teach. The Psalmist hid the Word of God deep in his heart so he could draw from it when the temptation to sin arose. It is so easy to take a casual approach to the study of the Word of God, and that is why I am taking this time and space to examine several scriptures, which confirm the importance of spending quality time studying and searching the scriptures. He went on to say, *"Thy word is a lamp unto my feet, and a light unto my path" (Psalm 119:105).* Without the Word of God, an individual is walking in darkness.

From the Pit to the Pulpit

Many people are looking for a pulpit from which to preach because preaching looks glamorous when a person is in a church or an arena, with many adoring fans listening to the message. When the Word of God comes to you in the pit, you realize that the world is your pulpit, and you don't need to be in a nice building with some dressed-up folks to preach and teach the Word. Make the homeless shelter your pulpit; make the prison your pulpit, as I did, and make the street corner or the bus station your pulpit. Believers have become too accustomed to congregating in buildings listening to one individual pontificate. We need to get out into the highways and the hedges and preach the Gospel of the Kingdom to the lost. The people in the pews should be trained to go out and make other disciples; instead, it appears that the paradigm is to learn to be the next great preacher or teacher. Jesus did not spend most of His time in the synagogue, and when He did spend time there trying to teach the religious leaders, they tried to kill Him. He told us to "go ye." He didn't say "stay there."

As soon as I came into the knowledge of the Lordship of Jesus Christ, I was ready to witness and share the Word. We have to be willing to go, but we must have something to take with us when we go so we will not be ashamed. We need a foundation in the Word that will stand against any religious opposition we encounter. I came in contact with people of many beliefs in prison who tried to tell me things contrary to what the Word said, but I would have none of it. What they came with their false teaching, I was able to draw on the well that was bubbling up inside of me. Only what is inside of you can come out of you, so get the Word in you so you can regurgitate it when it is necessary.

When I think of the pit from which He delivered me, I am motivated to go. I am not motivated by the money, by the fame, or any other perks that accompany the preaching and teaching of the Gospel. I want to share the Gospel with others because it introduced me to the real Jesus, and He changed my life. I am indebted to His Word and committed to spreading it far and wide. I concur with the Apostle Paul when he said, *"For though I preach the gospel, I have nothing to glory of: for necessity is laid upon me; yea, woe is unto me, if I preach not the gospel" (1 Corinthians 9:16)*. It is all about spreading the gospel because the gospel is the power of God unto salvation for all who believe. We must not have any hidden agendas or motives. Our sole motivation for preaching and teaching the gospel is to see souls saved and delivered from bondage. God have mercy on people who prostitute the gospel for material gain.

I know I have to live a chaste life, and that is not always easy because of the temptations that are out there, but the Holy Ghost in tandem with the Word will help me to triumph over every temptation.

When I fall, the Word lets me know that Jesus is faithful and will cleanse me and forgive me of all unrighteousness. *"Wherewithal shall a young man cleanse his way? By taking heed thereto according to thy word" (Psalm 119:9).* The words "a young man" do not only speak of a person from the age of infancy to adolescence; they also speak of someone who is not mature in the Word. Taking heed to the Word of God will not only cleanse an individual, it will mature them. The Apostle Paul told Timothy that, *"All scripture is given by inspiration of God, and is profitable for doctrine, for reproof, for correction, for instruction in righteousness: That the man of God may be perfect, thoroughly furnished unto all good works" (2 Timothy 3:16).* The Greek word translated *inspired by God* is *theopneustos* from *theos,* God, and *pneuma,* breath.

In his book, *The Basics: A Categorical Bible Study;* Gene Cunningham says, *"When Paul says that all Scripture is profitable, he uses a word that means advantageous, or beneficial. Then he lists four purposes for which Scripture is beneficial."*

1) **For Teaching**. *Didaskalia* means, *that which is taught, doctrine.* The Bible gives us the body of truth—the doctrine—upon which we are to base our perspective and make our decisions in life.

2) **For reproof**. *Elegchos* means *to convict of error and to rebuke.* The Holy Spirit uses the Word to show us where we have wandered off course.

3) **For correction**. *Epanorthosis* means *restoration to an upright or right state.* Along with the conviction that we are going the wrong way, the Word always sheds light on the right way. If we are humble before God, from the reproof will come a change in our attitude, which will result in personal action that sets us on course again.

4) **For training**. *Paideia* means *instruction and discipline given with the goal of raising a child to maturity.* The Bible

132

is a guidebook to lead us from spiritual infancy to spiritual maturity and beyond.

Whether you are a preacher in the pulpit of a church, with a large congregation, or an inmate in the pit of a prison, the Word of God will thoroughly furnish you with the things you need to fight the good fight of faith. God has supplied us with the Word, but we have to supply the motivation to study and learn what is written in His Word. We will not be able to plead ignorance if we neglect the Word because He has given it to us and given us instructions on how we should handle it.

There are many other scriptures that I can share with you that tell you the importance of the Word, but I will leave you with one more. Jesus told His disciples, *"Now ye are clean through the word which I have spoken unto you" (John 15:3).* Paul told Timothy of many of the ways in which the Word of God is beneficial; Jesus gives one benefit in John 15:3, which I think is the most important. The most important benefit is the Word's ability to cleanse us. The Blood of Jesus cleansed us so we do not have to deal with the ultimate penalty of sin, which is death, and the word cleanses us by teaching us how to keep ourselves unspotted from the world's system.

CHAPTER 10

A New Creation

Someone described salvation as the greatest miracle, and I agree. There is something awesome about the manner in which the Lord takes a sinner condemned to die, pardons that individual, and then prepares him to carry His Glory. Any condemned man would be happy just to receive a pardon or a stay of execution, but can you imagine the joy of the individual who received the pardon if, after being pardoned, his record is wiped clean and he is given the best of everything? That example pales in comparison to the transformation that takes place in the new birth when a sinner becomes a new creation in Christ Jesus and is invited to dwell in His Kingdom. When He finishes the work that He started in us, we will be a new creation. The Apostle Paul summed it up best when he told the Corinthian Church, *"Therefore if any man be in Christ, he is a new creature: old things are passed away; behold all things are become new" (2 Corinthians 5:17).*

A Renewed Mind

A new creation means we think, speak, and act differently. This is made possible as we endeavor to take on the Mind of Christ. In order for that process to take place, our minds must be renewed because thought precedes action. If an individual desires to change his actions and his attitude, he will have to be willing to change his thought patterns. Old thoughts do not die easily, so we have to continue to train our minds by thinking on things that are Godly. There are times when I am praying and out of nowhere, the vilest thought will enter my mind. When a wicked thought comes into the mind, we have to cast that thought down immediately. The thoughts we are willing to entertain are the thoughts upon which we will be tempted to act. When I received salvation in prison, I had no more desire for alcohol and no more desire for the street life because my mind was renewed. I would be less than honest if I said I lost all desire for carnal things. There are still some areas in my mind that desire things that are not pleasing to the Holy Ghost. That is why the mind must go through a constant renewal; if it does not, the new creature will fall back into old habits. In Romans, Chapter 12, the Apostle Paul gives the believer instructions on what we have to do to keep our minds and bodies from conforming to the world's paradigm. The Apostle said, *"I beseech you therefore, brethren, by the mercies of God, that ye present your bodies a living sacrifice, holy, acceptable unto God, which is your reasonable service. And be not conformed to this world: but be ye transformed by the renewing of your mind, that ye may prove what is that good, and acceptable, and perfect, will of God" (Romans 12:1-2).* He tells us to give our bodies as a present to God.

In times past, God dwelt in temples made by hands, but now He is dwelling in His new creation. Paul said our bodies are the temples of the Holy Ghost, and for this reason, we should not do anything we feel like doing with our bodies. I do not believe anyone in their right mind would want to dwell in a polluted house; in the same manner, God wants us to dwell in clean temples. Paul goes on to say that we should not be *"conformed to this world."* The Apostle Peter called us *"a peculiar people."* The Bible clearly tells us that a friend of the world is not a friend of God, and that is because this world's system is under the control of the devil. We know this to be a fact because all around us we can see the perversion. Some of the things coming into our homes through our televisions are unbelievable. As new creatures in Christ Jesus, we have to battle against these ungodly images that try to invade our minds in order to control how we act. We have to be non-conformists to the world's system. The Greek word for conformed is *suschematizo* (pronounced *soos-khay-mat-id-zo*). It means *to fashion alike or to conform to the same pattern.* When God instructed Moses to build the tabernacle, he was told to make it after the Heavenly pattern. By the shedding of His blood, Jesus Christ is making us new creatures who are tabernacles being constructed after the Heavenly pattern. The Apostle goes on to tell the believer that he has to *"be transformed by the renewing of his mind."* The believer will not be able to present a holy body to the LORD as a living sacrifice if there is no renewing of the mind. When we were slaves to sin in the world's system, there were strongholds set up in our minds, and these strongholds have to be torn down. The Greek word for renewing is *anakainosis* (pronounced *an-ak-ah-ee-no-sis*). It means *renovation*. Think of it as a messy construction site. The old building is being torn down to make way for the new one. A construction site is a messy place, but once the new building is erected, the mess gives way to beauty.

Your life might be a bit messy right now, but tell people to be patient with you because you are under construction. Paul says the renewing of the mind takes place when we are transformed. The Greek word for transformed is *metamorphoo,* and it means *to change or to transfigure.* This process can be likened to the process through which a caterpillar goes to become a butterfly. It is the transformation that is taking place in the life of the person who has accepted Jesus Christ as their Lord and Savior.

How we walk the Christian walk and talk the Christian talk in this life will be determined by the degree of transformation that takes place in our minds. It is impossible to discern the perfect, the good, and the acceptable will of the Lord without mind renewal. You know the adage "an idle mind is the playground of the devil." We have to keep our minds full of the Word of God, and we have to train our bodies by continuing to act upon His Word. In these last and evil days, the mind is and will be the battleground for spiritual warfare because the devil knows if he can attack the mind of the believer with lascivious, licentious, and perverse thoughts, he will be able to subject our bodies. As a new creation in Christ, we have to fight his encroachment against our minds on a daily basis.

One of the devices the devil will use against us is a spirit of condemnation. He loves when we play back in our minds the ungodly things we have done in our bodies. We must constantly remind ourselves that we are a new creation in Christ Jesus, and He is constructing us as tabernacles. There will be times when we will think and act in ways that are not pleasing to God, but we do not have to walk around in condemnation, dragging memories of past sins and transgressions like a ball and chain fastened to our ankles. There are many scriptures that tell us how to keep our minds strong in the Lord. In Philippians 4:8 Paul said, *"Finally, brethren, whatsoever things are true, whatsoever things are honest, whatsoever things are just, whatsoever things are pure, whatsoever things are lovely, whatsoever things are of good report; if there be any virtue, and if there be any praise, think on these things."* This scripture will help you to train your mind in the things of God, but you will have to do what it says. I know the honeys in the *Playboy* or *Penthouse* magazine might look good to the eyes, but that is not the thing you want to think on. If you struggle with pornography, then you should know that it is not wisdom to have the cable channels that beam this filth into your mind. Don't keep magazines in your home that feed your desire for perversion. Do not hang out in topless bars and nightclubs if you are trying to keep yourself chaste before the Lord. Meditate on what the Apostle told the Philippians. Think on the things that are true, honest, just, pure, lovely, and of a good report.

Satan is the accuser of the brethren, but as long as we have the mind of Christ, our actions will be pure. Satan's goal is to drag us back to the carnal mind so he can go before God and accuse us. It is nice to know that even when we mess up, we have the opportunity to repent; and when we repent, the accuser runs right into the blood when he tries to bring an accusation against us before God.

As a new creation in Christ, we are justified. In God's eyes, it is just as if we have never sinned. By Jesus' death on the cross and His resurrection from the dead, God has purged our sins and blotted out our transgressions. He has given us the opportunity to start a new life in Christ. We have to make the conscious decision to continue to live as a new creation. In the realm of the spirit, He has seated us with Christ in Heavenly places, but our bodies are still living in a fallen world, which tries to entice the old nature. Spiritually, we are a new creation in Christ, but our bodies have not been glorified so we have to continue to sanctify our selves by dying daily through the crucifying of the flesh. As a new creation, we have to turn from past behaviors and habits that fed the carnal nature. We have to have a mind that is focused on the Kingdom of God and not this world.

When people bring up my past, I tell them God has thrown my sins into the sea of forgetfulness to remember them no more. So, they are welcome to go fishing in the cesspool of my past if they desire. People love to remind us of what we used to do, but God has washed the slate clean via the blood of Jesus. We should live as new creatures in Him and not look at ourselves merely as sinners saved by grace.

The nature of people is to focus on the negatives. Peter is remembered as the person who denied Christ. David is remembered for sending Uriah to his death so he could sleep with Bathsheba.

One of my favorite stories in the Bible is the healing of Naaman, the leper. Naaman had an accomplished resume. *"He was captain of the host of the King of Syria, was a great man with his master, honorable, and by him the LORD gave deliverance unto Syria; he was also a mighty man in valour."* With that description, Naaman sounds like a candidate for man of the year, but 2 Kings 5:1 ends by saying, *"but he was a leper."* Leprosy was a dreaded contagious disease, for which I am sure Naaman would have traded all his accomplishments to get a cure. The words that follow the conjunction "but" cast an ominous shadow over all of Naaman's accomplishments. We all have a "but" in our lives. I am not referring to our posterior but to the things in our past, which the devil tries to bring into our future. You need to tell the devil to get out of your past because you are going to kick his "but."

Do not allow anyone to hang your past sins around your neck like an albatross. Misery loves company, and people would rather see you miserable than to see you walking as a new creature in Christ. The Apostle told the Corinthians that old things are passed away. I believe that means they are dead and should be buried. Out with the old and in with the new. People should be celebrating the new you in Christ, not trying to resurrect the dead man. However, we should not expect others to forget about our past transgressions if we are not willing to forgive and forget about them ourselves. It is extremely difficult to make forward progress when we are constantly looking back. At times, we can be our worst enemies. Stop beating yourself up over things that you cannot undo; once the milk is spilled and is out of the bottle, it is best to clean it up and move on. Why sadden yourself by dwelling on youthful indiscretions or bonehead mistakes you made as an adult?

I know some of us have done terrible things and wish we could undo them, but my dad always told me what his dad told him: *"You cannot take back a spoken word or a spent coin."* Once you know you have repented of the sin, then get it out of your mind and move forward.

Sometimes the people who were adversely affected by our actions will refuse to forgive us and will try to condemn us every chance they get, but you have to let them know you are truly sorry, and you are moving on because God has forgiven you, and you refuse to spend the rest of your life apologizing for something you did in the past. There are many people who are unable to get past their victim mentality, and that is a shame. The person who hurt them repented before God and has gone on with their life, but because of a spirit of unforgiveness and an unwillingness to let go of the past, that person lives in torment.

I have many things in my past about which I am not proud, but I refuse to live life being tormented by them. I have learned from the pain they caused me and others, and I use the experience to help make sound decisions. One of the things I like to tell people is this: "You must learn to get over people's opinions." It is what God says about us that is important. We must believe His report and not the report of people who do not have good intentions for us.

I remember witnessing to a childhood friend, and he kept reminding me of the times we hung out and partied; he kept reminding me that he knew me from my childhood. He knew his lifestyle was wrong, but instead of receiving the words I spoke to him, he constantly tried to remind me of the days we used to hang out and drank alcohol. Finally, I told him that he was talking about a dead man. He was trying to focus on my old man, who was under the control of a sin nature. He did not understand the fact that I was a new creation in Christ, and when the new me was born, the old me died. I was not going to allow anyone to resurrect the old man, especially after all the problems he'd caused me! I told him the old Fidel was dead and buried, so he was wasting his time talking about the actions of a dead man.

When the accuser of the brethren comes at you with past sins, just tell him and his minions that he is talking about a dead man—a man that was crucified with Christ. Take him to the cross by reminding him that Jesus paid the debt for that transgression when He died on the cross, and when He arose from the dead, you arose with Him as a new creation.

My friend stopped bringing up my past and eventually gave his life to Jesus Christ. He is now full of joy because of what the Lord has done in him. He finally came to the realization that if God has forgotten your sins, no one should use them to torment you, and you certainly should not torment yourself with them. As foresaid, learn to forgive yourself so you can flow in the peace of God.

There are many times when I feel a spirit of condemnation trying to attach itself to me. It happens when I think about how my irresponsible behavior brought suffering to my family. It is easy to get into a melancholy mood at that point, but I always make a conscious effort to look at what the Lord has done in me since that time. I constantly remind myself that God has forgiven me and has given me another opportunity, and all I need to do is be the best father and husband I can be at the present time. I cannot stress this point enough. Far too many people are plagued by the failures of the past. I have said this before: Yesterday has gone into eternity; tomorrow is not promised; but today is a gift, and that is why it is called the present.

There is no sin you have committed that is resistant to the Blood of Jesus once you are willing to repent. As soon as you repent, that sin is blotted out. The enemy loves to torment us with memories of our sins, but keep reminding him of the Blood. He hates the Blood because it is the thing that washes us of the filth with which he smeared us. God is awesome in that He just does not clean us up and leave us, but He is going to use us as a show piece of his grace and mercy throughout the ages to come. What a mighty God we serve! No one else could take something that is old and make something new and beautiful out of it. As terrible as our sins made us look and feel, our new man in Christ will be beautiful because in the end he will be radiating in the Glory of God. Jesus was able to despise the shame because of the joy that was set before him. The devil loves the rewind button, but God loves the play and the forward buttons. When the devil hits the rewind button of your sinful past, hit the fast forward button and show him how bright your future is in Christ. Hit the fast forward button and show him what his end will be. Remind him that you are heading to a place out of which he was cast; remind him that you have taken the lofty place he once had of covering the throne of God with worship.

Embrace your newness in Christ because He paid a hefty price to give you that newness. God did not send Jesus to die on the cross for us so that we can be stuck in the past. God's desire for us to walk in our new life in Christ can be measured by the price He paid for us. Meditate on the fact that He gave Heaven's precious treasure, His beloved son. We do God a disservice when we allow the devil to keep us looking back. I know I have a criminal background, but I am not a criminal because the old Fidel is dead, glory to God!!! I embrace the fact the Apostle Paul said, *"All things are become new."* The Apostle Paul uses the phrase "in Christ" because there is nothing old or dead in Christ. Since we are in Christ, we are in a place of perfection in terms of our position in Him. We still have to deal with the pitfalls of living in a sinful world, but we must continue to press forward to physically become what Christ has made us spiritually. It means there is no aspect of my old life or your old life that God will hold against us. It is as if we have been re-created. Please remember that it is a process, and we have to continue to walk it out in His word because our adversary is constantly trying to drag us back into past sins. One day, we will reach a place of total sanctification, but until then, we have to continue to submit to God and resist the devil so he will flee. Please remember what the Apostle told the Church at Philippi. *"That I may know him and the power of his resurrection, and the fellowship of his sufferings, being made comfortable unto his death; if by any means I might attain unto the resurrection of the dead. Not as though I had already attained, either were already perfect: but I follow after, if that I may apprehend that for which also I am apprehended of Christ Jesus. Brethren, I count not myself to have apprehended: but this one thing I do, forgetting those things which are behind, and reaching forth unto those things which are before, I press towards the mark for the prize of the high calling of God in Christ Jesus. Let us therefore, as many as be perfect be thus minded: and if in anything ye be otherwise minded, God shall reveal even this unto you" (Philippians 3:10-15).*

Salvation is not an end in itself but a means to an end. Salvation is the beginning of a journey of complete sanctification. There is more to our life in Christ than being saved and waiting for the rapture. The Apostle Paul was converted while traveling on the road to Damascus, and from the moment of his conversion, he followed the Lord with zeal and passion. He sacrificed everything he had gained as a Pharisee in order to know all he could about Jesus. Paul was not satisfied with just being saved, and we should not be either. In the natural realm, he realized that although he had received salvation through the finish work of Christ, he had not yet attained perfection. The Greek word for perfect, as Paul uses it, is *teleioo* (pronounced *tel-i-o-o*); it comes from a root, which means *complete, to consecrate, to finish, or to fulfill.* This is the man God used to write two-thirds of the New Testament, and wrought many miracles through him, but he never rested on his last accomplishment for Christ. His desire was to be all that he could be in Christ.

He made a conscious decision that we should all make. He decided to forget all the things pertaining to his old life as a Pharisee, a persecutor of Christians. In Bible terminology, to forget does not mean to fail to remember. It means no longer to be affected or influenced by something. He decided that he was not going to let his life as a past persecutor of the Church affect or influence the work he had to do for the Lord. Unlike other Pharisees, he refused to allow his old religious mindset to hamper or hinder his forward progress. Paul was a scholar in the law and accomplished many things as a Pharisee, but he refused to rest on his works from the past. Listen to what he wrote to the Philippians: *"...though I might also have confidence in the flesh. "If any man thinketh that he hath whereof he might trust in the flesh, I more..." (Philippians 3:4).* He was telling them that he had just as much right as anyone else to put trust or confidence in the flesh because of his accomplishments. He goes on to lay out his credentials by saying, *"Circumcised the eight day, of the stock of Israel, of the tribe of Benjamin an Hebrew of the Hebrews; as touching the law, a Pharisee; concerning zeal, persecuting the church; touching the righteousness which is in the law, blameless. But what things were gain*

*to me those I counted loss for Christ. Yea doubtless, and I count all
things but loss for the Excellency of the knowledge of Christ Jesus my
Lord: for whom I have suffered the loss of all things, and do count them
but dung, that I may win Christ" (Philippians 3: 5-8).*

We are living in times when men heap titles upon themselves
with very little accomplishments in Christ, but Paul gave up all that
he gained as a Pharisee for the privilege of gaining perfection in
Christ. Pharisees lived the good life because they were looked up
to by the people as strict adherents to the Law of Moses. There are
people in the body of Christ that get offended if you do not put their
title before their name when you address them. Paul's sole purpose
in life after his conversion was being complete in Christ. He knew he
had done a great deal of harm to Christians because of the zeal that
he had for the law. When he gained knowledge of the truth, he was
willing to lay his life on the line to spread that truth among the Jews
and the Gentiles.

Many believers allow themselves to be hindered from a bright
future because of a dark past. You have to forget about the past sins
that hindered you; forget about the fact that you did not become
what your parent or parents wanted you to be; forget about the
failed marriage or marriages; forget about the church hurt you
experienced at the last church; forget about the people who are not
willing to forgive you for the mistakes you made. Be like Paul, and
reach forth for those things that are ahead in Christ. You have to
reach forth by pressing because the devil will attempt everything to
keep you remembering the things that are behind. He used religious
people to constantly attack Paul and question his qualifications in
Christ. I press, in Greek, means I follow after; it has the connotation
of intense endeavor. The Greeks used the term to describe a hunter
eagerly pursuing his prey. He is not spending his time and energy
pressing towards things that pleased his flesh or religious works
to pad his spiritual resume. We must spend our time pursuing the
things of God that will survive the fervent heat when every man's
work will be tried by fire. Paul kept his eyes looking forward as he
pressed towards the mark. The word mark in Greek is *skopos,* and it
means *a goal.* Beloved, you have to have a goal that you want to attain
in Christ, and you must be zealous in your pursuit of that goal. Do not

allow yourself to be hindered by the slothfulness of those around you. You might be in a marriage where your spouse is not willing to press on to know the Lord, but you have to have a made up mind that says, "I will not stay where I am not complete in Christ at the present time." There are things in the flesh that may be holding you back, but please continue to press towards the ultimate goal. Be like the hunter who is relentless in his pursuit of his prey. Our prey is the goal, and we must stop at nothing to achieve it.

The goal is the prize, and the prize is the high calling of God in Christ Jesus. If there is a high calling, could it be possible that there is also a low calling? We will not get the prize just by showing up to church on Sunday, Saturday, or whatever day you go to church. We have enough common sense to know that we do not get a week's paycheck for showing up to work once a week. A student will not earn good grades by attending classes sporadically and doing very little studying, so why do we think we can attain perfection by hanging on the periphery of Christianity? There will have to be a commitment to discipleship, a commitment to intense fasting and prayer to crucify the flesh, and a commitment to studying and applying the Word of God to our lives. Unfortunately, many Christians are not prepared to press or make the sacrifices necessary to attain that prize of the high calling. Many of are too busy with secular pursuits, busy trying to live like the Jones. There are but so many hours in a day. When we spend a great deal of time, energy, and resources trying to attain material success, how much time do we have left to dedicate to things of God? Do not settle for a low calling; dedicate your life to walking in the fullness of Christ, and trust God to supply the things you need. Keep your eyes focused on the prize, and refuse to settle for anything less than God's best.

The prize of the mark of the high calling is not bestowed upon us because we are saved. Without salvation, we will never attain the prize, but it is not enough to confess Jesus as Lord and Savior and not press on as a disciple. When Jesus saved us, He rescued us from the wrath to come by the shedding of His Blood, but we have to press on to get to the high place in Him. Many are called but few are chosen because only a few are willing to pay the price that it takes to attain perfection in Him. The Bible instructs us to "By the truth," and this means we must be willing to pay the price to walk in the truth.

I have always felt in my spirit that there is no way believers who operate as casual Christians will have the same rewards as believers who are dedicated to press on to perfection. A boss will not promote an employee if he is slothful, so why do we think God will reward slothfulness? Many believers are hearing feel-good messages that allow them to remain comfortable in their mediocrity while having an expectation of receiving blessings from the Lord. Jesus made it clear that the unprofitable servant will have the little taken away from him because he was unwilling to invest his master's talent.

God gave Evangelist Cheryl Young a message entitled, dig it up. He told her that many Christians have hidden their talent, and He wants them to dig it up. God has given you something to invest in the Kingdom, and you must not allow religion to bind you and hinder you from using that thing for the Glory of God. What have you done with the talent he has given you? If you have buried it, please dig it up. It will take some effort, but that is why you are part of the chosen few. He knows you have the ability to press. If the Apostle Paul had to press, then we will not be able to attain perfection by staying on cruise control.

We have to identify ourselves with Him and not with the old man. I am not saying we should deny the fact that His grace has saved us from our sins. We have to identify with the new man and not the old one. Being a new creature means we have access to a new realm. Our sins kept us from enjoying His Glorious Presence and blocked our entrance into His Kingdom, but now our new life in Christ allows us access.

On a personal level, my life of sin put me in a pit, then a prison, but the Blood of Jesus Christ rescued me and gave me the access I needed to enter His Palace. I liken His Kingdom to a palace because Jesus is King, and He said his Father's house has many mansions. The palace or the Kingdom of Heaven is a prepared place for a prepared people, so our time spent on earth should be a time of preparation for entry into that prepared place. Our preparation process begins on the day of our salvation but does not end until He is finished preparing us and we are ready to take our place as part of the Bride of Christ. The book of Esther is a great example of the time and effort that goes into the preparation of a bride to meet her groom. Esther went through twelve months of purification, which included six months with oil of myrrh and six months with sweet odors.

The scriptures are clear in its description of what happens to an individual who is unprepared. There were five foolish virgins who had the door to the palace shut on them because they were not prepared.

The Bible tells the story of a king who held a marriage feast for his son and noticed that one of the guests did not have on the proper wedding garment, so he had the attendants bind him hand and feet and cast him into outer darkness. Believers should be given intensive teaching on the presence of God and His Kingdom because we are being prepared to live in His presence. We have to understand the difference between the Kingdom of God and the Kingdom of Heaven. It is comforting to know that as His new creation, we will have a new home, and that home will be in His Kingdom. The Apostle Paul said, *"For the Kingdom of God is not meat and drink; but righteousness, and peace, and joy in the Holy Ghost" (Romans 14:17).*

The Kingdom of God is the sovereign rule and reign of the Lord Jesus in the hearts and minds of His people. The ministry of the Holy Ghost is to testify of Jesus and to illuminate the Word of God in our lives so we can get to a place where the gifts of the Spirit are manifested. Many people have religion; they have the outward appearance of Godliness, but they deny the power. The power is the power of the Holy Ghost and the work of transformation that He is doing in us to get us ready to dwell in the presence of the Lord. Jesus spoke to many people about His Kingdom when he was on the earth, but many of them were spoken to in parables. *"And when he was alone, they that were about him with the twelve asked of him the parable. And he said unto them, Unto you it is given to know the mystery of the kingdom of God: but unto them that are without, all these things are done in parables" (Mark 4: 10-11).* For many people, the Kingdom of God is a mystery. The Greek word for mystery is *musterion* (pronounced *moos-tay'-ree-on*); from *muo*, which means *to shut the mouth; a secret or mystery.* Our English word "parable" comes from two Greek words that mean *to cast alongside (para-* alongside; *ballo -* to throw or cast). A parable is a story or figure placed alongside a teaching to help us understand its meaning. It is much more than "an earthly story with a heavenly meaning," and it certainly is not an "illustration," such as a preacher would use in a sermon. A true parable gets the listener deeply involved and compels that listener to make a personal decision about God's truth and his or her life. Jesus knew that many people followed Him because they wanted a miracle and not because they wanted to be a disciple. He spoke to those people in parables.

The word "kingdom" means, *a political or territorial unit ruled by a sovereign.* It is the eternal spiritual sovereignty of God or Christ, and it also represents the realm of His sovereignty. To gain access into the Kingdom of Heaven, we have to become new creatures because God's Kingdom is a spiritual realm. Carnal people cannot gain access to that realm. We cannot enter the Kingdom of Heaven if the Kingdom of God is not within us. When we allow the Holy Ghost to take up residence in us, He will help us to overcome our fleshly, carnal desires. Please be cognizant of the fact that this is a process, and the process will not be completed overnight—but once the process is completed, we will receive the promise of the LORD to dwell with Him in His Kingdom.

Jesus told his disciples, *"And I will give unto thee the keys of the kingdom of heaven: and whatsoever thou shalt bind on earth shall be bound in heaven: and whatsoever thou shalt loose on earth shall be loosed in heaven" (Matthew 16:19).* Keys in Greek is *kleis* (pronounced *klice*); it comes from the root *kleio* (pronounced *kli'-o*) and it means *to close, to shut up.*

You may be in a place right now that is not glamorous. It might be an apartment, a job, a sick bed, or some other place where there is no joy. Please remember that your final destination in Christ is greater than where you are at this present time. Your environment does not and should not dictate who you are and whose you are. If you are in prison because of a crime you committed, and you have accepted Jesus as your personal Savior, you are now a new creation in Him. Old things are passed away, and at some point, your environment will change because you are destined for His Kingdom. There may be days when you will not feel like a new creation, but please remember that feelings are deceiving. Remember the words of the Apostle John: *"Beloved, now are we the sons of God, and it doth not yet appear what we shall be: but we know that, when he shall appear, we shall be like him; for we shall see him as he is. And every man that hath this hope in him purifieth himself, even as he is pure"* (1 John 3:2-3). Someone said, "There is something on the inside working on the outside." I would like to add a correction to that line. There is someone on the inside working on the outside, and that someone is the Holy Ghost. When He completes His work in us, we shall be like Jesus.

CHAPTER 11

The Power of the Holy Ghost

The Holy Ghost is the third person of the Godhead and is active in the building of the Church of Jesus Christ. He is the power source of the life of every Spirit-filled believer. It is sad to say that His ministry is misunderstood, and sometimes not understood at all. I used the word His because He is not a force, and He is not a thing. He is God, the Holy Spirit. He works in tandem with the Word of God to accomplish the Father's purpose in the earth. They work together because *"the letter killeth, but the Spirit giveth life" (2 Corinthians 3:6)*. From the start of creation, you hear of the Spirit of God hovering over the face of the deep and God speaking His Word. When Jesus was baptized in the Jordan river, the Heavens were opened and God spoke. A dove, which is symbolic of the Holy Ghost, was seen coming out of Heaven and resting on Jesus. When you find someone or some denomination that has the Word but not the Spirit, you will probably experience a great deal of religious legality. On the other hand, when you see someone with the Spirit, but that individual is a novice in the Word, you will probably not see a great deal of balance in that person's life. The Holy Ghost empowers us to be witnesses for Jesus and helps us to understand the deeper truths of God's Word.

In *The Basics: A Categorical Bible Study* by Gene Cunningham, the author writes, *"The Holy Spirit is, like the Father and the Son, both personal and individual. Though all three members of the Trinity are equal and share the same divine essence (Isa. 6:8-9; Jer. 31:31-34; 1 Cor. 12:11; 2 Cor. 13:14), yet the works of each differ. The Holy Spirit was intimately involved in the work of Jesus Christ on earth.*

1. *The Holy Spirit was the agent of Christ's conception (Matt. 1:18).*

2. *The Holy Spirit's sustaining ministry to the incarnate Christ was prophesied in the Old Testament (Isa. 11:2-3, 42: 1-4; Matt. 12: 18-21).*

3. *"The Holy Spirit was given without measure to Christ (John 3:34).*

4. *"The Holy Spirit had a special relationship to Christ during Christ's earthly public ministry (Matt. 3:16-17, 4:1; Mark 1:12).*

5. *"The Holy Spirit provided the power of Christ's earthly ministry (Matt. 12:28; Luke 4:14-15)*

6. *"At the cross, the Holy Spirit withdrew from Christ. During the last three hours on the cross, the Holy Spirit did not sustain Jesus, who was in that time experiencing spiritual death (Matt. 27:46; Mark 15:34; Ps. 22:1).*

7. *"The Holy Spirit was actively involved in Christ's resurrection (Rom. 1:4, 8:11; 1 Pet. 3:18).*

8. *"The Holy Spirit provided the power for the resurrection ministry of Christ (Acts 1:2).*

9. *"As the Holy Spirit empowered Jesus Christ during His earthly ministry, so He empowers the body of Christ, the Church today through the filling of individual Christians" (1 Cor. 12: 7-13; Eph. 5:17-18).*

When Jesus was about to ascend to Heaven, He gathered His disciples together and told them to tarry at Jerusalem until they "be endued with power from on high." They wanted to know if He was about to restore the Kingdom to Israel; they did not understand that the plan of God was bigger than the Kingdom being restored to Israel. God, through Jesus, was about to start His New Testament Church with power and authority that would change the world. When they asked about the restoration, Jesus said, *"It is not for you to know the times or the seasons which the Father hath put in his own power (Exousia). But you shall receive power (Dunamis) after that the Holy Ghost is come upon you: and you shall be witnesses unto me both in Jerusalem, and in all Judea, and in Samaria, and unto the uttermost part of the earth" (Acts 1: 7-8).*

The word tarry in Greek is *kathizo* and it means *to set, to settle, or to sit down*. They were instructed by Jesus to settle down at Jerusalem until they received the promise of the Father. The word endued in Greek is *enduo* and it means *to array, or to clothe with*. Remember, Joseph was given a coat of many colors by his father. His brothers stripped that coat from him, but Pharaoh arrayed him in vestures of fine linen. The Prodigal son was given a robe by his father.

God wants to array His sons with the glorious power of the Holy Ghost. *"And when the day of Pentecost was fully come, they were all with one accord in on place. And suddenly there came a sound from heaven as of a rushing mighty wind, and it filled all the house where they were sitting. And there appeared unto them cloven tongues like as of fire, and it sat upon each of them. And they were all filled with the Holy Ghost, and began to speak with other tongues, as the Spirit gave them utterance." (Acts 2: 1-4).*

The disciples followed the instructions of Jesus and received the promise of the Father just as He said they would. The promise was that they would be clothed with the dunamis of the Holy Ghost. The word *dunamis* in Greek means *miraculous power, ability or strength*. What was the purpose of this power? Was it to sit in church buildings every week preaching to the choir? Absolutely not. The power was given to the believer to be witnesses for Jesus. The Greek word for witness is *martus* (pronounced *mar-toos*). It means *a martyr*. A martyr is someone who is willing to die for his or her belief. We see the evidence of this witnessing as soon as the disciples were endued with the dunamis of the Holy Ghost from on high. The disciples came out from the upper room speaking in a tongue other than their common vernacular. There were devout Jews at Jerusalem from the surrounding nations, and they heard the disciples glorifying God in their own language. Some of the men began to mock, so Peter stood up with the eleven, lifted up his voice with boldness, and began to preach repentance in Jesus' name for entrance into the Kingdom of God. This is the same Peter who denied Jesus and cussed someone out when Jesus was arrested. Now, clothed with the Holy Ghost, he is emboldened to speak.

The Bible says, *"Now when they heard this, they were pricked in their heart, and said unto Peter and to the rest of the apostles, Men and brethren, what shall we do? When we get out from behind the four walls and witness to people in the power of the Holy Ghost they will be convicted."*

There should be more teaching on the ministry of the Holy Ghost. He came to empower the church for witnessing, so if the church is not willing to witness, then the dunamis will not be manifested. The Holy Ghost ministers to the church, but He also has an assignment to the world. Concerning that assignment, Jesus said, *"And when he is come, he will reprove the world of sin, and of righteousness, and of judgment: Of sin, because they believe not on me; Of righteousness, because I go to my Father, and ye see me no more; Of judgment, because the prince of this world is judged. I have yet many things to say unto you, but ye cannot bear them now. Howbeit when he, the Spirit of truth, is come, he will guide you into all truth: for he shall not speak of himself; but whatsoever he shall hear, that shall he speak: and he will shew you things to come. He shall glorify me: for he shall receive of mine, and shall shew it unto you" (John 16: 8-14)*. The Holy Ghost was not sent to testify of Himself but to guide the believers into all truth concerning Jesus. He illuminates the Word in the life of the believer.

I remember sitting in a revival service in Mount Olivet Gospel Church, and Evangelist Clifford Simmons was preaching. He started singing a song with the words, *"fire fall on me, at the day of Pentecost, fire fall on me."* It felt like the fire was really falling on me. I jumped out of my seat and started praising God as He filled me with His precious Holy Ghost. Prior to that filling, I was a timid believer who kept quiet in church. Once I received the baptism of the Holy Ghost, I began to praise God with boldness, and to witness with great boldness.

No Holy Ghost, no power. Let God be true, and let every man be a liar. We cannot be effective witnesses for Jesus without the Holy Ghost. If the disciples who walked and talked with Jesus needed to wait for the promise of the Father so they could be endued with power from high, then every other believer must be endued with that same power in order to fulfill their ministry on the earth. I am not saying you cannot witness for Jesus without the Holy Ghost. I am saying that without the baptism of the Holy Ghost, you will not have the power and the authority. God is a promise keeper, and He has promised the believer the gift of the Holy Ghost. If you have not been baptized in the Holy Ghost, then ask the Father and He will give Him to you; but remember, He is not coming to dwell in you so you can be sedentary or a pew warmer. He is coming to empower you so you can go into the highways and the hedges and call people to repentance. You might be afraid of rejection right now, you might be timid when it comes to witnessing to others about Jesus, but when the Holy Ghost takes up residence in you, all that will change. Just look in the book of Acts and you will see a picture of the disciples before they received the Holy Ghost and after they received His power.

Acts chapter 3 tells us how Peter and John went up together into the temple at the hour of prayer. It was the ninth hour, and nine is symbolic of the Holy Ghost. A lame man was in front of the temple begging for alms. Peter told the man to rise up and walk in the name of Jesus, and the man got up and started leaping. Peter used the occasion of the healing of the lame man to witness, and that infuriated the priests, the captain of the temple, and the Sadducees. They were upset because Peter and John preached resurrection from the dead in Jesus' name. They arrested Peter and John, but because they had the power of the Holy Ghost, they were not intimidated. The Bible says, *"And when they had set them in the midst, they asked, by what power, or by what name, have you done this? Then Peter filled with the Holy Ghost, said unto them, you rulers of the people, and elders of Israel, if we this day be examined of the good deed done to the impotent man, by what means he is made whole; Be it known unto you all, and to all the people of Israel, that by the name of Jesus Christ of Nazareth, who you crucified, whom God raised from the dead, even by him doth this man stand here before you whole"* (Acts 3: 7-9).

Peter did not attempt to take credit for himself because he knew it was the power of the Holy Ghost and the name of Jesus that caused the lame man to be healed. Notice the religious leaders' question. They asked by what power and by what name? If the church wants to see people healed, delivered, and set free, we have to get back to preaching in the name of Jesus and in the power of the Holy Ghost. In so many churches, it is all about the leader. There is a spirit of Hollywood and a spirit of show business. People preaching feel-good messages that do not bring conviction to the heart of the listeners. The gospel has to be preached because it is the gospel that is the power of God unto salvation. There are plenty of secular motivational speakers around, if that is what people want to listen to. Jesus empowered His church with the Holy Ghost so we can make a difference on the earth. The Five Fold ministry was given to the church to perfect the saints for the work of the ministry. The ministry that was given to the church is the ministry of reconciliation—reconciling lost sinners back to the Lord Jesus Christ.

There is nothing wrong with blessings and prosperity, but that should not be the focus of the Church of Jesus Christ. He said if we seek the Kingdom first, then He will add the things we need. We need to follow the paradigm of Jesus that He established when He was on the earth. He trained His disciples, then He sent them out to cast out devils and heal the sick. It appears that many modern day church leaders are more interested in keeping the people in the buildings listening to their great, sermonic oratory skills. What about Jesus' command to go into all the world and make disciples? In our churches today, only a small percentage are willing to go out into the world. The majority are not taught to go; they are influenced to stay. What is the purpose of having people sitting in the pews for years? The church should not be about membership; it should be about people being empowered by the Holy Ghost, trained, then sent into the community to heal the sick and cast out devils. Jesus said first Jerusalem, then Judea, then Samaria, then the uttermost parts of the world. There is nothing wrong with going to Africa and other nations, but we must not neglect the fact that the neighborhoods outside of our church doors are in need of the gospel. We need Pentecost at any cost. We need the demonstration of the power of the Holy Ghost in our churches. We don't need celebrities in the pulpit giving us points on how to receive material blessings. We do not need slick sermons that make us feel good. We need to turn down our plates and get back to the altar. We need to cry out to the Lord of the harvest and ask Him to send forth laborers into the fields. We need to stop making demigods out of our favorite preachers. We are living in the age of the Laodicean church, which is the church described by Jesus in Revelation Chapter 3, increased with goods but lukewarm.

We have been hearing glowing messages of prosperity over the last decade, and now we are increased with goods but lack power. Why aren't we seeing the miracles of the early church today? They didn't have the silver and the gold, but they had the "such as I have" that Peter spoke about. The "such as I have," is the power of the Holy Ghost, and the desire to go into the world and make disciples. We do not need leaders that sit on grand stages in oversized chairs while their loyal adoring church fans fawn at every word they speak. We should give honor to whom honor is due, but things have gotten out of control. The leader of the flock should be the one leading the people into the community to take back territory from the devil. Study the life of Jesus and tell me if He spent most of His time in the temple or in the streets ministering to prostitutes, wine bibbers, and other sinners. Study the life of the disciples and tell me if they spent most of their time in the temple; as a matter of fact, the Lord sent persecution to spread them out when they were shut up in Jerusalem.

Judgment begins in the house of the Lord, and judgment is coming because we have allowed a spirit of Babylon to enter the church. Jesus will not stand idly by while sinners perish in their sins; while we are shut up in our members, family and friends, churches singing and ministering to one another. Christ receives sinners, and we need to understand that sinners are not going to flock to our churches. We have to get out there and compel them to come in so the Lord's house can be full.

Please do not allow yourself to settle into religion. God has saved you and given the Holy Ghost for a reason, and the reason is for you to walk in demonstration and the power of God. We don't need that demonstration among other believers. The sinner trapped in darkness needs to see the power of the Holy Ghost so they can be delivered. Jesus came to destroy works of the devil, and that is exactly what He did when He saved you and me and filled us with the Holy Ghost. He wants to destroy the works of the devil in the life of other individuals, and that is why He commanded us to go. If your church does not have a plan of evangelism to win the community for Christ, then maybe God wants you to start it. If they do not have a prison ministry, maybe it is time for you to start one. Be willing to come out of your comfort zone, and the Lord will use you to do great things. Jesus came out of His comfort zone for us. There is no place in this universe that can be compared to Heaven, but He left the riches of Heaven, came to earth, and became poor for you and me. He wants to use us as His ambassadors to win the lost, but we have to be willing to come beyond the place where we are.

When the Lord broke the darkness of my life on March 6, 1991, I could not wait for the cell door to open so I could witness to other inmates. The prison was my Jerusalem, and I made full proof of the ministry of reconciliation when I was there by starting the Bible study. I had no ambition to be the next wonder. I had no desire or ambition to be a preacher. I found a savior, and I wanted the men around me to know that whom the Son sets free, he is free indeed. I knew the miraculous transformation I experienced, and I knew God could do the same for other people. My friends thought I had professed Jesus Christ because I wanted to get parole. They thought that I would go right back to a life of drinking and partying as soon as I got out of prison. What they did not understand was the fact that I had a Divine visitation from the Lord on March 6, 1991, and He transformed my life. As much as I missed my wife and kids, my focus at that time was allowing God to finish the work He'd started in me in the prison cell.

God allowed me to get first parole even though when I got the sentence, there was no parole for people who were convicted of a felony. I was released a new creation in Christ three years to the day that I was sentenced. Remember, the number three is symbolic of resurrection and Divine completion. I came to England a spiritually • dead man bound by alcoholism, perversion, and filled with a lot of anger and bitterness. I left a new creation in Christ Jesus. Elmcor Alcohol and Drug Rehabilitation Center and Rikers Island Prison were my Judea because those are the places I went to share my testimony. I went to Elmcor and Rikers with a ministry team from Mount Olivet Gospel Church. I know I was rough around the edges then, but the team was very patient with me. When the Holy Ghost instructed me that I needed to go to Elmcor more frequently, I started a weekly

Bible study there. The drugs that I dealt helped to destroy many lives, and now I wanted to reach as many people as I could with the gospel.

I enjoyed going to the rehab and the prison, and I witnessed the power of Jesus through the Word and the Holy Ghost to change the life of the individuals who were willing to receive Him. Eventually I began to experience Samaria and the uttermost parts of the world when I went on mission trips to Jamaica and when the Lord opened doors for me to preach and teach the gospel all over.

I was very zealous for evangelism when I returned home, but there were some things the Lord wanted me to do as a responsible husband and father. I had a great deal of work to do in that area because of my failures as a husband and father before I went to prison. I had been gone from home for three years, so I had to work on becoming the best husband and father I could be. The Lord spoke to me and told me that I had to do what was necessary to make sure my children were helped spiritually and materially. I realized that it was not wise to want to travel all over the world to minister when things were not right at home. I went to church with my wife and kids and did my best to instruct my kids in the things of the Lord. I witnessed God do a great work in them.

Words cannot adequately describe the love I have for King Jesus because of what He did and continues to do for me. I often think of the many individuals with whom I ran the streets who did not make it. They did not get to see their kids graduate from high school and college. They did not get to see them get married or have their first child. I owe everything to the Lord because of what He has done for me. I know beyond a shadow of a doubt that my life is not my own because Jesus redeemed me from the hand of the enemy by the shedding of His precious blood. I want to continue to do what pleases Him by allowing the fruits and the gifts of the Spirit to manifest in my life. I want to teach others of His goodness. I want others to experience the richness of His blessings, and I will do everything in my power to spread the good news.

A Grain of Wheat

When you love Jesus, you are willing to roll up your sleeves, get in the trenches, and allow God to use you to deliver souls and make disciples. When Jesus saved me, I had no idea He would use me in the manner He has. I was totally satisfied with witnessing in the prisons and alcohol and drug rehabilitation centers. The idea of standing in a pulpit to preach was the furthest thing from my mind. God knew that He would use me in such a way, but I had no idea. When I used to drink and mock the preachers in front of my wife, she told me that one day I would be preaching the gospel. I laughed. As I look back over my life from the days of teaching Bible study to the precious disciples in the prison on the Isle of Sheppy, to the interview on Christian Television that allowed me to share my testimony, to the grace God has given me to write books, I am humbled by the fact that God would use me for His Glory. This is the reason we must not give up on people. We must continue to believe in God for their salvation. It does not matter how sinful their life is at the present time. God can take an alley cat and turn him into an aristocrat and a citizen of His Kingdom.

While traveling to North Carolina to preach, I received a phone call from my sister. She informed me that a lady named Linda wanted to speak with me. When Linda got on the phone, she shared a story with me that brought me to tears and reaffirmed why the Lord saved me in prison and why my life is dedicated to spreading the gospel. Linda got on the phone and said, "Minister Fidel, this is Linda. You gave me a copy of your book, _Don't Birth An Ishmael In The Waiting Room,_ last year, before I went to New Jersey. I have a nephew in Jersey who was selling drugs and getting into a lot of trouble. I showed him your book and told him, this pastor went through a lot of the things you are going through, but worse. I sat on the porch and read your book to him, and the Lord changed his life. He was stabbed to death by his girlfriend and at the funeral, the pastor told the audience how God had changed his life and He could change theirs, if they gave Him the opportunity. Many people came to the altar to give their hearts to the Lord." When she told me he was saved, and then stabbed to death by his girlfriend, tears began to well up my eyes, but the Holy Ghost reminded me of John 12:24. Jesus said, _"Verily, verily, I say unto you, except a corn of wheat fall into the ground and die, it abideth alone: but if it die, it bringeth forth much fruit. He that loveth his life shall lose it; and he that hateth his life in this world shall keep it unto eternal life._

158

If any man serve me, let him follow me; and where I am, there shall also my servant be: if any man serve me, him will my Father honour."

I was saddened when I heard that he'd lost his life, but I rejoiced in the fact that God, in His infinite wisdom, allowed him to receive salvation before he died. In our finite minds, we cannot always comprehend why things happen the way they happen, but we can trust God and know that the Judge of the whole earth will do right. God will allow things to happen for His Glory, and we have to put our complete trust in Him. Out of the young man's death came eternal life for all the individuals who came to the altar to repent.

When Linda shared the story with me, I was further motivated to press on and spread the gospel. There are many other sons and daughters out there who have their minds blinded by the god of this age, and God wants us to take the light of the gospel to them. The light of the gospel can shine in the darkest of hearts, but we must be willing to go because souls hang in the balance. Every soul is precious in the sight of the Lord, and that is why the Bible says, *"There is joy in Heaven over the one sinner that repents."* Jesus talks about the shepherd who leaves the ninety-nine sheep to go after the one. God's desire is that none should perish, but that all should come to a saving knowledge of Jesus, and He wants to use you to reach the one. It does not matter where you find yourself at the present time. You are just one prayer away from God's plan for your life, but that prayer has to be the prayer of repentance if you are not saved or if you are backslidden. You might be walking with the Lord but not walking in your calling. You can turn today and surrender your will to Him so He can use you to reach others. Jesus laid down His life for you, and He wants to use your life to reach others.

I consider myself a dead man who was pardoned. I was dead in trespasses and sin, but the Lord Jesus took my place in the death chamber. I owe Him everything and so do you because He took your place, too. He did not save us just to take us to Heaven; He saved us so He could use us on this earth to testify of His Goodness so others can be set free.

CHAPTER 12

Placed for a Purpose

Purpose is the reason for which something exists, is made, or is done. We were created to worship the Lord and to live lives that bring Him glory. Sin entered our world, separated us from our purpose, and plunged us into a pit of despair. Jesus shed his blood for our redemption when he was crucified on the cross; He has given us the opportunity to be his disciples. Our discipleship has a two-fold purpose. He disciples us to prepare us for the palace, which is synonymous with His Kingdom, and He disciples us so we can help people who are going through things out of which He has brought us. When Joseph arrived at Pharaoh's palace, He was able to give Pharaoh the answer to his dream, which led to his promotion. The purpose of his promotion was not for him to live a life of ease in the palace; on the contrary, it was to allow him to help his family, the Egyptians, and the surrounding nations during the time of famine.

God did not bring you and me to His church so we could become religious bench warmers. He has delivered us and brought us to the body to use us to bring others. Jesus declared, *"And other sheep I have, which are not of this fold: them also I must bring, and they shall hear my voice; and there shall be one fold, and one shepherd" (John 10:16).* The pit, Potiphar's House, and the prison prepared Joseph for his purpose in the palace. If you are saved today, it means at one time you were not of His fold but you heard His voice, repented, and He brought you into the fold. Every time I have an opportunity to speak a word of encouragement to someone in prison, someone on drugs, or someone trapped in a place of bondage similar to the place from which the Lord delivered me, I consider it a privilege and an opportunity to operate from the place of purpose. The palace or the place of purpose is the place where we operate in our divine assignment once Jesus has given us the victory over the pit. The little maid in 2 Kings Chapter 5 was a captive in the house of Naaman the leper, but she was placed there for a purpose. Her purpose was to speak words that would send Naaman to the Prophet Elisha to be healed and restored. She did not allow her environment to hinder her testimony concerning the prophet of God.

I received a letter several months ago, and it was from an inmate on Florida's death row. As I read the letter, I could not help but wonder how difficult it must be to deal with the battle in the mind when you are in a dark place like death row. As I began to read the letter, I realized that the brother was able to mentally transcend the darkness and the pit of despair of death row because Jesus was dwelling in his heart.

He wrote to me because he had seen my interview on Christian Television. I went on TBN to talk about my books, but the Holy Ghost told me to share my testimony of how the Lord delivered me from the prison. I am glad I obeyed because many people, including Paul, the brother who wrote me from death row, heard the testimony and were blessed. For me, it was more important for the people viewing the program to hear my testimony—how Jesus turned my life around in prison and set me free. The TBN studio was a place of purpose, where God placed me to talk about my deliverance from the pit of prison. He did not place me there to speak flowery words; He did not place me there for people to see how well I was dressed. He placed me there as an instrument of His Divine purpose.

As I read Paul's letter, I could not help thinking that, based on my past life, it could have been me on death row. I thought about the fact that I was actually on death row when I lived a life without Jesus Christ. As far as God is concerned, all sinners are on death row, because the wages of sin is death. Instead of death, He gave me the gift of life through Jesus Christ.

As I read his letter, I remembered the days when I was in prison, and the joy that filled my heart when a letter came from home. I understood the importance of having a connection to the outside world when you are in prison for years. The importance becomes greater when a person is on death row and has exhausted all his appeals. As I read Paul's letter, I was overcome by the grace and the mercy of the Lord. He saved me in the prison, and now He was using me for the purpose of ministering to other prisoners.

I wrote him and sent him a copy of my book, _Mercy and the Sufficiency of Grace_. I try to send as many books into the prisons that I can. I want the person in the pit of prison to know that if Jesus delivered me, He can deliver him. I want him to know there is no pit deep enough, dry enough, dark enough that He is not able to pull him out, quench his thirst, and shine His light in there. Paul was blessed by the book and blessed by the fact that I took the time to write him with my own hand. Our schedules may be hectic, but we should never be so busy that we are unable to reach out and touch someone with the love and compassion of the Lord Jesus Christ.

He shared with me how the Lord was using him to minister to others on death row. Death row is a dark pit, but it can also be a place of purpose once Jesus is invited in. Jesus is the only one who can bring life out of death, light out of darkness, and joy out of misery. _"He turns our mourning into dancing; He gives us the garment of praise for the spirit of heaviness."_

The Lord has his soldiers in diverse places. He has hidden ones all over the world. They are graced to be in places where others cannot or will not go. They have turned their prison environment into a place of purpose. They have not allowed it to be a pit, but a place of divine purpose and assignment. I believe Paul has exhausted all his appeals, but I know he has the peace of God, which passes all understanding. I know that peace will guard his heart and his mind. When a man is willing to surrender to the Lord, He will use him as a vessel of honor. God does not see as men see. He sees through the eyes of love, kindness, forgiveness, grace, and mercy.

The fact that Paul is ministering to people on death row and people on the outside through letters is evidence to me that God shines His light in the darkest places, and uses whomever He chooses for His Glory. My brother called me from USP Big Sandy and told me that the inmates are waiting on my new book because my other books encouraged them. What joy those words brought to my heart, that

God would use me to be an encouragement to others. My brother's words gave me the motivation to start writing the manuscript for this book. It is not being written for fame or fortune. It is being written to encourage individuals who are in a pit, written to encourage them to hold on, and to cry to Jesus for deliverance. It is written to encourage individuals who have been delivered from a pit to remember others who are still there. Written to encourage them to let their light shine so men can see their good works and glorify the God of Heaven.

It was a joy for me to write Paul and to encourage him. The Lord did not save us just to deliver us from sin and to take me to heaven. Salvation is not an end in itself; it is a means to an end. The end is for the Glory of God to be manifested in and through us. The more we yield to Him, the more His glorious light will shine. We have to know our assignment. We have to understand the calling on our lives.

I went to the pit of prison for the crime I committed, but I was placed there for a purpose. When I was arrested and remanded to Wormwood Scrubs and Brixton prison, I had no idea that one day, the Lord would use what I had experienced to help others. Say yes to Jesus, and He will deliver you and transform the pit into a place of purpose. The place of purpose was the palace for Joseph, but it was the home of a leper for the little maid. For Moses, it was leading the people out of Egypt through the wilderness in preparation to enter the Promised Land. Their purpose for entering the promise land was not for them alone, but so heathen nations could see God's Glory on them. On many occasions, they aborted their purpose because they adopted the principles of the heathens around them. Wherever your place, allow your walk with the Lord to impact the atmosphere. Before he could be anointed over all Israel and Judah, David had to endure the attempts on his life by King Saul. He had to live in the wilderness and in the cave of Adullam. He became so distressed that he went to live in the land of the philistines. He had to endure the burning of Ziklag. *Ziklag* means *winding*, and it speaks of the ebbs and flows, the highs and lows we will encounter on the road to the palace, or the place of purpose. He had to endure the capture of his wives, and the wives and the children of the men who were with him. When he came to the place of purpose, which was the palace, he was able to reach down and help Mephibosheth, the grandson of King Saul, the man who repeatedly tried to kill him.

Mephibosheth was dwelling in a place called lo-debar. *Lo-debar* is defined as *the place of no pasture*. Random House Webster's Collegiate Dictionary defines the word pasture as, *"An area of ground covered with plants suitable for grazing of livestock; grassland."* A farmer or a shepherd is in dire straits when there is no pasture for his animals. Jesus is the good Shepherd, and He leads to good pastures. The road may be rough and tough, but never give up because in Jesus, we will find the green pasture.

David was a shepherd, so he understood how egregious it was for Mephibosheth to dwell in Lo-debar. Jesus declared, *"I am the door: by me if any man enter in, he shall be saved and shall go in and out, and find pasture" (John 10:9)*.

Mephibosheth was living in a dry place. He was not living the life of the grandson of a former king. He was in such a place because his nurse dropped him while fleeing after the death of his father and grandfather on the battlefield. When he fell, both of his feet became lame. He was only five years old at the time. Many of us have been dropped by a caretaker and are in Lo-debar because the emotional pain of being dropped has crippled us and affected our walk with the Lord. We may have been dropped inadvertently, but the pain and the effects are still difficult to deal with. If you were dropped by someone you loved, someone you trusted, if you are in Lo-debar at the present moment, do not give up—the King is on the way. He is looking for you. He will not drop you. Jesus declared, *"My sheep hear my voice, and I know them, and they follow me: And I give unto them eternal life; and they shall never perish, neither shall any man pluck them out of my hand. My Father, which gave them me, is greater than all; and no man is able to pluck them out of my Father's hand" (John 10:27-29)*.

David never forgot the kindness of Mephibosheth's father, Jonathan. Once he got to the place of purpose, he went down to Lo-debar to look for any member of the previous royal family so he could show him kindness for Jonathan's sake. David could have taken revenge on the remaining member of Saul's family, but he chose to show kindness instead. He traveled a long, arduous journey to get to the palace, but it was that journey that made him the man after

God's own heart. I heard an evangelist say, "It takes a pulpit to make a preacher, but it takes an altar to make a man of God." When David found Mephibosheth, he told him, *"Fear not: for I will surely shew thee kindness for Jonathan thy father's sake, and will restore thee all the land of Saul thy father; and thou shalt eat bread at my table continually" (2 Samuel 9:13).*

When Isaac was living in a land of famine, the LORD appeared unto him and told him not to go down to Egypt, but to sojourn in the land of which He spoke. The LORD promised to be with him, to bless him and to give him and his seed all the land. God gave him such a great promise because Isaac's father Abraham obeyed the voice of the LORD and kept his charge, His commandments, His statues, and His laws.

David's words to Mephibosheth paints a beautiful picture of restoration. David could have kicked back in the confines of the palace and relaxed. Instead, he chose to go down to Lo-debar. Jesus could have stayed on His throne in heaven, but He chose to come down to earth to seek and save the lost. David remembered the days of his pit experience. He remembered the days when he was in a place of no pasture and had to ask the fool Nabal for food for his men. Lamentations 1:6 declares, *"And from the daughter of Zion all her beauty is departed her princes are become like harts that find no pasture, and they are gone without strength before the pursuer."*

There is a great principle in this story. The fact that Mephibosheth was lame in both his feet is symbolic of an individual who does not have a walk with the Lord Jesus. His nurse dropped him when he was five years old, and five is the number of grace. Through grace we are saved through faith, and not of ourselves; Mephibosheth needed grace to pull him out of Lo-debar, the pit of no pasture, and take him to the palace, the place of purpose. By the grace and mercy of God, David was able to survive his own Lo-debar experiences, and unlike Saul he had a heart for the people.

David's purpose for going down to Lo-debar was to show him kindness. He went as a king to restore the things Mephibosheth had lost. King Jesus will restore the things we lost when Adam sinned. He will restore marriages; He will restore lost children; He will restore sick bodies back to health; He will restore the sinner and the backslider back to fellowship. David went down to bring Mephibosheth up to his table to eat bread continually. This is a beautiful picture of what the Lord Jesus desires to do for sinners dwelling in Lo-debar, those who are dwelling in the pit of despair and degradation, those trapped in the prison of perversion and promiscuity. Jesus traveled through His own Lo-debar on His way to the cross to suffer a brutal, agonizing death, but it was for a purpose. The cross was His place of purpose, because the cross was the place where He took our sins upon himself. Psalm 23 encapsulates this point beautifully. In it, David declared, *"The LORD is my shepherd; I shall not want. He maketh me to lie down in green pastures: he leadeth me beside the still waters. He restoreth my soul: he leadeth me in the paths of righteousness for his name's sake. Yea, though I walk through the valley of the shadow of death, I will fear no evil: for thou art with me; thy rod and thy staff they comfort me. Thou preparest a table before me in the presence of mine enemies: thou anointest my head with oil; my cup runneth over. Surely goodness and mercy shall follow me all the days of my life: and I will dwell in the house of the LORD for ever."*

David wrote this beautiful Psalm to describe the manner in which the LORD will protect his sheep by leading them to green pastures. When David was young, he led his father's sheep in the wilderness to find pasture. When he was in the cave of Adullam, he led the people who were distressed. When he grew older, he led Mephibosheth to the table to eat bread, to be sustained continually. On the road to the place of purpose, he endured many pits, many prisons, but he was always sustained by Jehovah Jireh, the God of provision. This is the reason he was able to declare, *"The LORD is my Shepherd, this is the reason he was able to declare in Psalm 37:25, "I have been young, and now am old; yet have I not seen the righteous forsaken, nor his seed begging bread."*

Here is something extremely important that we must understand: Jesus wants to deliver us from the pit of no pasture. He wants to bring us to His table to nourish us with bread. There is a purpose, and the purpose is not for us to get lazy and slothful. He wants to bring us out of our pit, out of our prison, out of our Lo-debar, so He can use us to reach down and pull up the Mephibosheths of this world. We are not blessed just to be blessed. He has blessed us to be a blessing.

Jesus is the good Shepherd. He leads the sheep to green pastures so He can feed them. You see a beautiful picture of this in the feeding of the five thousand. *"And he commanded the multitude to sit down on the grass, and took the five loaves, and the two fishes, and looking up to heaven, he blessed, and brake, and gave the loaves to his disciples, and the disciples to the multitude" (Matthew 14:19).*

Remember, Mephibosheth was five years old when he was dropped, and he became lame in his two feet. Five for grace and two for witness and separation. Jesus commanded the multitude to sit down on the grass. David declared, *"He maketh me to lie down in green pastures."* Jesus commanded the multitude to sit down on the grass. Jesus gave the loaves to the disciples, and the disciples gave them to the multitude. This is why Jesus commanded us to make disciples and not church members. Disciples will get the loaves from Jesus and feed the multitude. The revelation is this: Jesus is the loaf being distributed by the disciples to the multitude because He declared, *"Verily, verily, I say unto you, Moses gave you not that bread from heaven; but my Father giveth you the true bread from heaven. For the bread of God is he which cometh down from heaven, and giveth life unto the world. Then said they unto him, Lord, evermore give us this bread. And Jesus said unto them, I am the bread of life: he that cometh to me shall never hunger; and he that believeth on me shall never thirst" (John 6:32-35).*

Please hear me. The sinner is in spiritual Lo-debar where there is no pasture, and God wants to use us to bring them to the table of Jesus Christ where they can be restored and where they can eat bread continually. In order for this to take place, we must allow Jesus to take us to the place of purpose. He will do it when we repent of our sins and ask Him to come into our hearts and be the Lord of our lives. He will do it when we refuse to allow people, places, and conditions to keep us in a state of depression and despair.

Jesus knows about the place of no pasture. He was born in a manger, the place where animals dwelt, because there was no room at the inn. I am not talking about the Holiday Inn, because He did not come into this world to vacation. He came to destroy the works of the devil and to set the captives free. His birth in a manger meant He could identify with everyone, no matter the lowliness of their birth.

You may have had a rough beginning. The circumstances surrounding your birth may be akin to that of someone born in a manger, but God has a plan and a purpose for your life.

The story of David and Mephibosheth is a beautiful picture of that plan. Wherever you are at the present time, He wants to take you higher. The Apostle John was on an island called Patmos. He was banished there for the Word of God, and for the testimony of Jesus Christ. It was on that island that he declared, *"I was in the Spirit on the Lord's Day, and heard behind me a great voice, as of a trumpet."* In Revelation 4:1 he declared, *"After this I looked, and behold, a door was opened in heaven: and the first voice which I heard was as it were of a trumpet talking with me; which said, come up hither, and I will shew thee things which must be hereafter."* The Prophet Ezekiel was sitting by the river Chebar captive in Babylon. While the other captives hung their harps on willow tress and were weeping, Ezekiel looked up and saw visions of God.

For you, Lo-debar may be a prison cell. It may be a wheelchair. It may be the fact that you are trapped in a body that is debilitated by an infirmity. Whatever the condition, whatever the pit, look up in the realm of the Spirit, look up through fasting, prayer, and worship, and you will hear the voice of the trumpet; you will see visions of God.

When David summoned Mephibosheth and told him he would show him kindness, Mephibosheth's response showed that he was in a place of low self-esteem. He said to David, *"What is thy servant, that thou shouldest look upon such a dead dog as I am" (2 Samuel 9:8).* Lo-debar will sap your strength and kill your self-esteem if you allow it to do so. The pit will drive you to despair if you allow it to do so. The prison will be a place of persecution if you allow it. Jesus will elevate your mind and take you to the palace, the place of purpose—if you allow Him. The choice is yours. You have to decide if you are going to allow your environment, your circumstance, your situation to make you feel like a dead dog. He came that you may have life and that more abundantly. With Jesus on board, the place of no pasture can become like an oasis in the desert.

Jesus endured the cross and despised the shame for us, so we must be willing to bear our own cross. We have to come to the realization that it is not just about us but about what Jesus desires to do in and through us. He ministered to hated tax collectors, people possessed by devils, and drunkards. When His disciples tried to keep women and children away from Him, He would insist they be brought to Him. There are many people perishing in the pit of despair, and all they need is someone who is willing to reach down and pull them out. We are the hands and the feet of Jesus on the earth. We have to walk in our purpose and show people the Love of Jesus.

I am so grateful that the Lord pulled me out of the pit of my Lo-debar, which was the prison next to the pig farm. I know my life has to be dedicated to doing His work. It has to be dedicated to evangelism, and it has to be dedicated to perfecting the saints for the work of the ministry of the Lord Jesus. I was bought with a price. I was redeemed for a purpose. I know in my heart that I am His bond servant. If He had not pulled me out of the pit of drug dealing, drunkenness, whore-mongering, fornication, and adultery, I would not be here to write this book. I am sure I would be in the grave if He had not rescued me. *"To whom much is given much is required."*

When He gave His life for me, He gave me everything, and I owe Him everything. He gave His life for you, and you must make the decision to forsake all to follow Him. When you read the Psalms written by David, you see a picture of the deep love he had for the Lord. It was a love that stemmed from a heart, which was grateful for the many times the Lord delivered him from the pit of despair and from his enemies.

Study the scriptures, and you will see that God used ordinary men and women to accomplish extraordinary things. Many of them had to endure hardships and trials. He is still looking for ordinary men and women to use to accomplish extraordinary things. The Apostle Paul wrote two thirds of the New Testament, but instead of gloating he describes himself by saying, *"And I thank Christ Jesus our Lord, who hath enabled, me for that he counted me faithful, putting me into the ministry; who was before a blasphemer, and a persecutor, and injurious: but I obtained mercy, because I did it ignorantly in unbelief. And the grace of our Lord was exceeding abundant with faith and love which is in Christ Jesus. This is a faithful saying, and worthy of all acceptation, that Christ Jesus came into the world to save sinners; of whom I am chief"* (2 Timothy 1:12-15).

The apostle called himself the chief among sinners. He did not feel special or entitled because of all the things Jesus used him to accomplish. He was grateful that the Lord would use him after all the things he had done to the church. It is that brokenness and humility that allowed him to endure the suffering he endured for the gospel's sake. We have to endure hardship for the sake of the gospel. God used trials and tribulations to break the flesh of the people He used for His purpose, because if they were not broken, they would take the glory for themselves. God is looking for living vessels who are will to be broken for His purpose.

Servants

God is not looking for the next wonder; he is looking for the next servant. He is looking for the next Esther who will say, *"If I perish I perish."* He is looking for the next Paul who will say, *"Lord, what will thou have me to do?"* He is looking for the next person who will say, like Jesus, *"not my will but thine be done."* Are you that person? Are you willing to forsake all to do the work of the Lord? Say yes to Jesus and be a servant; He will use you to be His minister, and will get glory out of your life. He will reach out to you wherever you are. He will come to the pit for you; He will come to the prison; and He will come to Lo-debar.

The Purpose of the Minister

We have to teach the Biblical definition of the word minister. When you look at the incident in the Bible where the mother of Zebedee's children came to Jesus desiring a special position for her sons, you can learn that, no matter what our title or position, we are called and must be willing to serve. *"Then came to him the mother of Zebedee's children with her sons, worshipping him, and desiring a certain thing of him. And he said unto her, what wilt thou? She saith unto him, Grant that these my two sons may sit, the one on thy right hand, and the other on the left, in thy kingdom"* (Mark 20:21-22).

There is nothing wrong with a mother desiring a good position for her sons, and what better position could a person have than to be seated on the right hand or the left hand of Jesus? Jesus' response to her and the example He gave the disciples when He found out they were indignant over what Zebedee's wife did is a great example for all ministers of the gospel in how they should operate. Jesus let them know that they would have to be able to drink from the cup He would drink from and be baptized with His baptism. He was telling them that such lofty positions did not come without a great price, and the price is suffering. *"And when the ten heard it, they were moved with indignation against the two brethren."* I believe they were indignant because they wanted the position for themselves. Jesus told them that, *"the Princes of the Gentiles exercise dominion over them, and they that are great exercise authority upon them but it shall not be so among you: but whosever will be great among you, let him be your minister; and whosoever will be chief among you, let him be your servant: Even as the Son of man came not to be ministered unto, but to minister, and give his life a ransom for many."*

In the world's system, a person's stature and influence is often determined by how many people over whom they have authority. In the church, a person's stature and influence should be determined by his willingness to serve others. Jesus said if a person desired to be great, then he must be willing to minister. The word minister as the writer uses it in Matthew 20:20 does not mean someone who is able to preach, teach, or sing. The Greek word for minister, as it is used there, is *diakonos* (pronounced *dee-ak-on-os*), and it means *to run errands, a waiter at table or in other menial duties.* Jesus is telling the apostles that if they wanted to be great, then they should be willing to run errands and wait on tables. Jesus went on to say that the person who wanted to be chief should be a servant. The Greek word for servant is *doulos* (pronounced *doo-los*), and it means *a slave or a bondservant.* This is astounding when you think about the fact that Jesus is speaking to the apostles, who would transform their world with the gospel. He had to get arrogance and ambition out of them. I love it when Jesus concluded by telling them, *"the Son of man came not to be ministered unto but to minister, and to give his life a ransom for many."* The Greek word used by Jesus to describe Himself as a minister is *diakoneo* (pronounced *deek-ak-on-eh-o*), and it also means *an attendant, servant, to wait upon menially or as a host.* When someone comes to you throwing their title around in arrogance, you should ask them if they are a minister, then explain to them that minister does not mean someone who is arrogant, full of pride and puffed up, but someone who is a servant, someone who is willing to do the menial work. People who were broken in the pit will be humble enough to serve.

Please do not sit around waiting for someone to validate you. Jesus has called you from the pit to the place of purpose so He can work in and through you. He has placed gifts and talents inside of you that He wants you to use for the building of His Kingdom here on earth. *"Ye have not chosen me, but I have chosen you, and ordained you, that ye should go and bring forth fruit, and that your fruit should remain: that whatsoever ye shall ask of the Father in my name, he may give it you" (John 15:16).* He has placed former pit dwellers in His church for a purpose. Study the lives of the people of the early church, and you will see that they had all things common. They were led by the Holy Ghost. They did the work of the Kingdom, and God wrought miracles through the hands of the apostles and added daily to the church, such as should be saved. God has not changed: *"He is the same yesterday today and forever."* He is still in the miracle working business. He is looking for vessels who will avail themselves to Him.

Let's yield to the power of the Holy Ghost so the fruits and the gifts of the Spirit can be manifested in our lives. When our lives are submitted to the Holy Ghost, He will tell us how to live and walk out the profession of our faith. We must stand fast in the liberty wherewith Jesus Christ has made us free and not be entangled in the yoke of bondage. Religion binds, but a true relationship with the Lord Jesus will set us free. The Apostle Peter said, *"But ye are a chosen generation, a royal priesthood, an holy nation, a peculiar people; that ye should shew forth the praises of him who hath called you of darkness into his marvelous light" (1 Peter 2:9).*

Be true to the gospel of the Lord Jesus Christ. Walk worthy of your calling in Him. Allow Him to use you to be a witness and a blessing to those in need, and never forget that what you do in secret, He will reward openly.

Some of us are like gold taken out of a mine, placed in the fire to remove the impurities. Some are like the olive being crushed so the precious oil can come forth. Wherever you are at the present time, know that you are precious and priceless, like an expensive diamond.

You may be in the rough at the present time, but God wants to pull you out, polish you, and use you as a reflection of His Glory. Like a precious diamond that is cut, God has to cut us. Diamonds are not formed overnight.

In her article "The Origins of Diamonds," eHow contributing writer, Jenni Wiltz wrote, *"Diamonds originated deep within the earth as simple atoms of carbon. The carbon was compressed into a rock and carried to the earth's surface by volcanic magma. Diamonds are the hardest gemstones on earth, with a 10 out of 10 rating on the MOHS hardness scale. Their three-dimensional chemical structure is what makes them so sturdy, and so practical for daily wear. Diamonds are formed beneath the surface of the earth, in the rocky portion between the crust and the core known as the mantle. Temperatures in the mantle can be a high as 1,000 degrees centigrade. When combined with extreme pressure (up to 50 kilobars), these conditions transform the naturally occurring element carbon (chemical symbol C). Carbon atoms are compressed by the temperature and pressure and layered on top of one another, forming a diamond. The stone is carried to the earth's surface through volcanic eruptions."* The forming of a diamond is a beautiful picture of how the life of the believer is formed by Jesus. Diamonds are formed beneath the surface of the earth, in the rocky portion between the crust and the core. I love the fact that the place of formation is called the mantle. Jesus is the rocky portion; He is the core and the center of our lives. When His work is complete in us, we will be sturdy; we will be able to wear the mantle He will give us. One thousand-degree temperatures are very hot, and fifty kilobars of pressure is extreme, but that is what makes the diamond the hardest gemstone on earth. We cannot wear the mantle of the Lord Jesus if we are not able to withstand the heat, the pressure, and the volcanic eruptions.

The devil thought the pit would be the place of our destruction; he thought the prison would be the place of our demise; he thought the heat of the fire and the extreme pressure would dissolve and disintegrate us. He did not understand that the heat and pressure would be used by God to create layers of strength, which would transform us into something strong and purposeful. In the manner that a diamond is carried to the earth's surface through volcanic eruptions, we refuse to perish in the volcanic eruptions that take place in our lives. They give us strength and fortitude and help us to rise from the pit, to the surface. We rise out of the ash heap like Job; out of the pit, Potiphar's house, and the prison like Joseph; out of the cave like David; and out of the grave like Jesus.

Like a diamond, we have a three-dimensional makeup. We are spirits, we have souls, and we live in a body. We received this makeup from The Father, the Son, and the Holy Ghost. They keep us sturdy and give us the ability to function and survive the daily wear and tear of life. When the Father, the Son, and The Holy Ghost complete the work they have begun in us, we will be a perfect ten.

You may be languishing in a pit, but do not allow yourself to sink into a pity party. The heat and the pressure are forming layers of thickness on you for the purpose God has called you. As you experience eruptions in your life, do not faint. Look up; the Lord is waiting for you with outstretched arms, waiting to pull you up to the surface. He will not leave you in the furnace a moment longer than necessary.

Allow Him to elevate your mind. Thought precedes action, so you must begin to free your thoughts from the place of captivity. The body has to follow the instructions given to it by the brain, so make up your mind that your Kairos time for deliverance from the pit of your present place is now. If your mind is in the pit, if it is in Lo-debar, there will your body be also. It does not matter how long you have been there; the important thing to understand is that this is your season and your hour of power. Keep looking up because you cannot see what is above you if you keep your head hung down low. Dry your eyes; weeping has had its day in your life. It is time for the joy of the Lord to be your strength. It is time to mount up with wings of eagles. It is time to arise from the place of hopelessness to the place of holiness. It is time to arise from the place of depression to the place of your divine assignment. It is time to arise from the place of misery and melancholy to your place of ministry.

If you are a backslider, then please take this opportunity to pray a prayer of repentance and get back into fellowship with the Lord. If you have not accepted Jesus into your heart, please take this opportunity to pray now. Say, *"Heavenly Father, I am a sinner. I thank you for sending Jesus to die on the cross for my sins. I repent of my sins, and I ask you, Lord Jesus, to cleanse me now. Come into my heart and be the Lord of my life. Fill me with your precious Holy Ghost, and use me for the building of your Kingdom. Amen."*

If you have come to the Lord, you are now a new creation in Jesus Christ. You are a babe, and you will need the milk of His Word to survive. A seed has been planted in you, and you will have to nourish it for it to grow. Get into a church fellowship where the Word of God is taught, the Lord is worshipped, and the people have a mind to work. Commit yourself to learning and living by His Word. May the Love of the Father Yahweh, the grace of our Lord Jesus Christ, and the sweet communion of the Holy Ghost be with you as you travel on the narrow road of this Christian Journey.

Agape
Bro. Fidel
www.fideldonaldson.org

BIBLIOGRAPHY

Arthur, Kay. The Peace & Power of Knowing God's Name. Colorado Springs, Colorado: Water Brook Press, 2002

Conner, Kevin J. Interpreting The Symbols And Types: Portland, Oregon: City Christian Publishing, 1992

Cunningham, Gene. The basics: A Categorical Bible Study. Bigelow, AR: American Inland Mission, Inc. 1990

Random House Webster's Collegiate Dictionary. New York: Random House, Inc. 2000

Sproul, R. C. The Character of God: Discovering The God Who Is. Ann Arbor, Michigan: Servant Publications, 1995

Strong, James. The New Strongs Exhaustive Concordance of The Bible. Nashville: Thomas Nelson, Inc. 1995

CPSIA information can be obtained
at www.ICGtesting.com
Printed in the USA
FFOW02n1157090418
46172325-47387FF